To: Kathl

Thank _YOU_ for supporting!

Continue to bless and
inspire the masses!

Much love,

Heal

Your

Heart

ALSO BY DR. EDDIE M. CONNOR, JR.

Purposefully Prepared to Persevere

Collections of Reflections, Volumes 1-3:
Symphonies of Strength

E.CON the ICON: from Pop Culture to President
Barack Obama

Unwrap The Gift In YOU!

Heal Your Heart

Discover How To Live, Love, And Heal From Broken Relationships

Dr. Eddie M. Connor, Jr.

Heal Your Heart and other books by Dr. Eddie M. Connor, Jr. may be purchased for business, educational, or sales promotional use. For information, please e-mail the Administrative and Markets Department: info@eddieconnor.com

FIRST EDITION

Library of Congress Cataloging-in-Publication Data has been applied for.

ISBN-13: 978-0692302941

ISBN-10: 0692302948

10 9 8 7 6 5 4 3 2 1

Printed in the United States of America

To my beautiful and beloved mother, Dr. Janice K. Connor who devotedly raised myself and brother, Elijah. A retired educator of 30 years, who worked tirelessly as a single parent mother. She currently travels the globe as an author, conference speaker, evangelist, and brings tranquility to lives as a counselor.

Your faith, dreams, hope, and belief in me has propelled me this far and is the catalyst to push me further into the future.

Thank you for everything that you have done and continue to do. I love you, Mom!

CONTENTS

Heal

Your

Heart

FOR MORE ON
HEAL YOUR HEART

VISIT:
WWW.EDDIECONNOR.COM

INTRODUCTION

Healing For Hurting Hearts

Open your mind and take this literary journey with me. While reading *Heal Your Heart*, you may laugh, shed a tear, or crack a smile. As long as you think, more concretely and succinctly about your life, then this book has served its purpose.

For years, I have been writing this book in my mind. My experiences, pain, healing, hope, and purpose have brought me to this point to share on this topic with you. Indeed it took courage, patience, and fortitude to coalesce life-long experiences and place them within this medium, of literary material. So I wrote what I needed most. As I was writing, I was healing. As I was typing, I found therapy. As you're reading, you will begin receiving wisdom, to *Heal Your Heart*.

As you open this book, you are opening the deep places within my heart and soul, that seek to speak life into your life. It doesn't take being a relationship expert, psychologist, or marriage counselor to talk about love. It takes courage to walk in love and express your truth about love. The greatest expression of truth is rooted in the tests and trials, that one has overcome. We all have the ability to share about love, because we are human beings who have a desire to express and receive love.

Healing is not always an event, sometimes it's a process. The process of being healed takes time, patience, and commitment. You can be dealing with scars and wounds, while healing from them at the same time. One of the greatest consolations, is that I'm comforted in knowing, there is a purpose through the process, a message through the mess, and a testimony through my test.

Everyone desires to fill a void in their life, that inner-hole within. Sometimes we go through life on auto-pilot, you know, existing instead of living, to the point that we don't even recognize our own emptiness. Have you ever been emotionally, psychologically, relationally, or spiritually broken? Just limping through life. Smiling on the outside, hurting on the inside to where you cry yourself to sleep, night after night.

"DAMAGED GOODS"

Sometimes we have become so numb to pain, that it hurts to be happy. Some people try to fill the void and hurt in their heart with drugs, alcohol, money, fame, sex, cars, clothes, and commodities. The aforementioned, is the stuff we classify as "The finer things," but it's all vanity. We just end up emptier than ever. Little do we recognize that we all seek love differently, in a multiplicity of ways.

Love fills the void in our lives. It begins with embracing God's love and personifying self-love, whereby we can express love to others. This kind of love empowers us to press past hurts, disappointments, abuse, neglect, skeletons in our closets, and the frightening things we fight to overcome. Each one of us, has a "Fragile, do not drop" label on our lives.

We have all been dropped in various ways, whether by an absentee father, disappointment, or life's situations. From the toughest of us, to the most sensitive, there are places in our lives that need healing, in order to live our best life. You may have been dropped and damaged, but God can repair and fix your heart.

The strength discovered in life, derives from how you handle what you go through. I'm a believer that 10%

of life is what happens to us, 90% is how we proactively move forward, as a result. There are things that you may never get over, they just have to be managed. More than going through, you have to GROW through every hurt and disappointment! Be empowered through this literary treatise to live, laugh, and love on a greater level.

SPEAK TO MY HEART

This book *Heal Your Heart* speaks to remedying the issues, that we deal with from within. Sometimes our heart, echoes the words of the 70s soul singer, Rose Royce, "Just a vacancy, love don't live here anymore." A heart shattered, broken in pieces, and void of love, due to hurt.

You may say, "I've been hurt and I don't know, if I can ever love again." Yes we've been hurt, but we have also hurt others too. I'm sure you have heard the saying, "Hurt people, hurt people." There is much truth and pain, in the simplicity of the statement. Simply because, if the hurt within has not been healed, it will flow through one's life and afflict others. On the contrary, healed people, heal people and loving people, love other people. What flows through you is a direct reflection of what is in you.

As you read *Heal Your Heart,* I believe that you will discover powerful truths, to lift your life and those who surround you to another level. Whatever the challenge, this book will position you on the path of purpose, to find opportunity in every obstacle. Anticipate a renewed, refreshed, and resilient mindset as you read each chapter.

To every beautiful sister who reads this book, I want you to lift up your head and look into the mirror of your soul, to discover your inner peace, value, and beauty. My brothers, be encouraged and strengthened in knowing, that there is a purpose for your life. No amount of money or material possessions, can determine your value.

You, yes YOU are priceless. Know your worth. Appreciate who you are. Embrace your gifts. Live with purpose, love yourself, heal your heart, and reveal your greatness within!

Reach out and let me know, how this book has helped you or someone that you know. I often say, "The revolution will not be televised, it will be online and I don't want you to miss it." Log on and connect with me, at www.EddieConnor.com, join me there for more information and inspiration.

As you know, social media is the norm these days. I want you to be mentally, spiritually, and relationally F.I.T., so connect with me on Facebook, Instagram, or Twitter @EddieConnorJr, and use the hashtag #HealYourHeart.

I'm looking forward to inspiring you on this journey. May you discover healing, joy, peace, and love, to live your best and blessed life!

CHAPTER 1

It Begins From Within

T he best investment that you can make is not in the stock market, not in a *Louis Vuitton* account, a business venture, or a fancy car. The best investment that you can make, is in YOURSELF!

Many times, we compensate for what we lack on the inside, by accumulating a lot of things on the outside. The thoughts, "If you get that new dress or pair of shoes, then you will feel better about yourself." Yes, that may be true but it's only momentary happiness.

Material possessions don't satisfy long-term. You know how it goes, it's trendy today, out of style tomorrow.

It's a façade of happiness, but it's not real joy. You just become an emotional spender, an emotional eater, or thrill seeker who continues chasing but finds life unsatisfying. A life of consuming without investing, will leave you bankrupt.

A SENSE OF SELF

This world we live in, is designed to stimulate and cater to our five senses. Everything is tailor-made to stimulate your sense of touch, taste, smell, sight, and hearing. To live by sensual perception, minimizes your growth and causes you to live impulsively. To live by psychological and spiritual conception, enhances your growth, causing you to live abundantly.

To continually look on the outside, to find relief within, can drive you crazy. The spirit, the soul, the heart is so precious and priceless, that nothing outwardly can provide the peace that you need inwardly. Many times we have allowed people to hurt, damage, bruise our hearts, and trample over our dreams. When we no longer see the good in ourselves, we surround ourselves with those who don't see the good in us either.

You are not the pain of your experience. Don't allow painful experiences to define you. Use them to refine you and birth a spirit of resilience, within you. Your future destination, is greater than your past situation. When you value yourself, you will surround yourself with those who value you. How can you expect somebody to love you, if you don't exemplify and express love within yourself?

LOOKING IN ALL THE WRONG PLACES

So many times, we make the mistake of holding on to what we should let go. We even make bad decisions, by reaching for things, that were not any good for us in the first place. We often take our bruises and scars, to people and places, as if to say, "Will you love me?" Those same people that we go to, are sometimes bruised and scarred themselves.

How can we find healing from people, who are hurting themselves and tending to their own wounds? We make the mistake, of looking for people to fill the void in our lives, when we must find a place of tranquility and hope within.

Let's be honest, we can the best at playing the blame game. We point to others, blame others, and make excuses for ourselves because of others. You know how it goes, "If this didn't happen I would be here, if I was raised this way, if so and so didn't do this." When you point the finger, there are always more pointing back in your direction, being placed in your face. It doesn't end with them, before it begins with you.

THE BLUEPRINT

People will treat you, by the way you allow them to. When you take inventory of your life, you are able to set standards, goals, principles, and values for living. You give people a blueprint, of how to treat you, by the way you treat yourself.

Your life is a magnet. If you're nasty, mean, angry, and bitter that is what you will attract and as a result, you will be treated as such. On the flip side, when you operate through self-love, a positive mindset, and actions that express those qualities, your life and the people in it, will begin to mirror those attributes.

NEVER BITTER, ALWAYS BETTER

The peace you seek, the love, joy, success, and quest for a better life, begins with you. Begin to discover, the greater good in you. Yes, the situation may have been ugly, you may have been abused, betrayed, or mistreated but something good, can still come out of a bad situation. Even if it's nothing but a testimony, that you survived and now you share it to help somebody else, then it was all worth it. Something beautiful, can arise out of an ugly situation.

Don't allow yourself to become ugly and bitter, because of it. Become better as a result of it. Forgive so you can live. Anticipate better and refuse to be bitter, by remaining positive in the midst of negative situations. In order to do that, it takes a committed will and a heart, that may have been hurt, but is pressing towards healing each day. It begins from within!

CHAPTER 2

Cancel My Subscription... I'm Through With Your Issues

As you read this chapter, I want to impress upon you, to embrace a spirit of optimism and victory. Everything bad that you have experienced, is still going to work out for your good. I don't want you to give up or throw in the towel. I do want you to realize, that the bigger the battle, the greater the blessing.

You have a purpose, you have life, and since you have life, that's the greatest opportunity to live, laugh, and love on another level.

SILENT SCREAMS

There is a story of a very rich man, who lived in a mansion and owned all kinds of elaborate paintings, fancy cars, and statues. Yet out of everything he owned, his prized possessions were his exotic fish, that swam in his luxurious in-house aquarium. His exotic fish, were some of the most beautiful sea creatures, from all 4 corners of the world. One night as he was on his way to bed, as was his custom, he fed his fish before he went to sleep.

This particular night, after feeding his exotic fish, the rich man adjusted the temperature of the aquarium. When he woke up in the morning, he was startled to see that all of his exotic fish had floated to the top of the tank and died, because of the excessively warm temperature of the aquarium. All of a sudden, rather than throwing up his hands in rage and eulogizing his fish, he asked himself, "I wonder did the fish scream at night and I didn't hear it?"

As you're reading this particular book, maybe you have been screaming, but nobody was receptive enough to hear it. Maybe you were silently screaming and no one was listening. All they could see was your makeup on the outside, yet they're blind to your pain on the inside. All they could witness, was how sharp your outfit was, but couldn't assess the temperature of a cold heart, that was void of warmth and love.

CLOSED HEARTS, OPEN WOUNDS

Dr. Cornel West declared, "We have deodorized the funk of our issues, we've perfumed our pain, and masked it with makeup." Have you ever been in a state of mind, where you found yourself smiling on the outside, but saddened on the inside? We would call that "Putting up a front" because we don't want people to know, that we don't always have it together. The social media or photography terminology for that would be "Using a filter," to counterbalance how we really feel, look, or think. Oftentimes we use personal filters in our lives, to color in the gray areas and hide our flaws. We have a propensity to alter ourselves on the outside, seeking to cover what we're dealing with on the inside. Sometimes we deal with issues that nobody knows about, struggles, setbacks, and circumstances that are too painful to mention.

Our hearts become closed doors, when there's nobody to share our issues with and open up to. Sometimes the hurt within, has ensued to such a degree, that you've pushed the pain of the memory in the back of your mind. Mentally perplexed because of the hurt, abandonment, abuse, and shame.

Oftentimes, our lives become much like the fish in the aquarium. The temperature of our hurt, pain, and issues has been turned up and now we find ourselves swimming in a cesspool of circumstances. Sometimes life, becomes a pool of pain and you're screaming for relief, but nobody hears you.

I can't hear your scream and I can't hear your voice, as you read this book. However, I do believe that God will use these words, to speak victory into your life, through healing, restoration, and overcoming power. Be encouraged, Psalm 118:17 declares, "You shall not die, but you will live and declare the works of the Lord."

A KNOCKDOWN, ISN'T A KNOCKOUT

Begin to adopt the attitude of a fighter. Yes, you may have been knocked down, but it happens to everybody. We all get knocked down, at some point in our lives. However, a knockdown becomes a knockout, when you stay down. Get up and get back in the fight!

I CANCER-VIVE

Personally, I know what it's like to fight and be the one screaming, yet seemingly nobody hears me. I know what it's like, to be in a fight and wanting to wave the white flag, capitulate, and give up. I almost died battling stage 4 cancer at the age of 15, but my dear mother reminded me that the prefix of the word "Cancer" is can.

God pre-fixed my fight, in order to give me the victory to win. Philippians 4:13 affirms, "I can do all things through Christ that strengthens me." Your struggle, strength, and victory is pre-fixed. Just hold out and hang in there, because in the end you will win!

You will revive your dream and resurrect your purpose. You're not going to only be delivered, but you will be healed. All bets are off, this is straight no chaser, raw, real, relevant, and uncut unadulterated truth. Despite the pain of the past, realize that God is healing the broken places in your life, mind, and heart. He is the only one who can give you peace, from life's broken pieces.

SEE BEYOND WHAT YOU SEE

As you read and mentally digest this information, discover a greater place of inspiration. Even now, your vision for your life is being restored. It's been suggested that "Having sight, without vision means you're still blind."

Don't you believe that there's more to your life, than what has been? You're called to be greater, do greater things, and live on a greater level. You're beyond the mediocre and mundane. There's more that you are to experience and achieve. Stay motivated through the process.

A negative state of mind, will trap you in a state of sickness, by suffocating your dreams and visions. When you get to a place that says, "I'm sick and tired, of being sick and tired," then you won't settle for mediocrity and mess. You will do more than survive, you will begin to thrive!

Begin to mentally break out of the box, live, think, and move freely. You have to walk in freedom, because you can't live aimlessly and void of purpose. Refuse to be sad, bad, and mad. Refuse to live your life, barely making it. You're too gifted to have less and think less of yourself. Begin to live life more abundantly. Refuse to be angry about what didn't work out, or who didn't treat you right.

Stop subscribing to mental junk and issues that should be discarded! A junk filled mind is worse than an email inbox, filled with junk mail. Send negativity a notice that says, "Cancel my subscription, I'm through with your issues." Don't subscribe to mess, when you were born to live blessed! Extra, extra read all about it. Cancel my subscription…I'm through with your issues!

AND THE AWARD GOES TO

You're too blessed to be stressed and associate with people, who bring junk and mess. When you really want better for your life, you will cut off negative people, drama, and dream killers. You won't live your best life, until you let go of drama, anger, bitterness, and strife. Give it an eviction notice, you may not know where it's going, but it has to leave your heart and mind.

I've come to the realization that some people are like soap operas, they're just filled with drama. If life were like the Academy Awards, I'm sure that you could think of somebody who deserves the title of best actor/actress, because of all their drama. They're deserving of a Daytime Emmy, for all of the drama they keep up, day after day. As you let them go, you will see that the drama leaves right along with them. God allows some people to walk out of your life, to make room for the right people to walk into your life.

Your responsibility is to press forward and not run back, to place them in your life, after God has moved them out of your life. It's your job to let them go, so you can grow. Stop holding on to people that have let you go. Start letting go of negative people who are holding on to you, because they will hold you back from your destiny and purpose.

You can't keep doing permanent things with temporary people, simply because doing permanent things with temporary people leaves you with permanent scars. The place to begin healing your heart, is to understand that there is a blessing in this lesson of letting go. You have the patience and preparation to pass the test.

LIFE IS SIMPLE MATH

On your journey, make sure that you have people in your life who are adding to you, not subtracting from you. There are people who only come into your life to take. Just taking your power, draining you of your peace, constantly complaining, and gossiping. Please believe me, if they talk about other people to you, they will talk about you to other people. Like they say, "If they bring a bone, they will take a bone."

One of the most important decisions that you will ever make, are the relationships that you choose to align yourself with. Whether it be friendships, business, dating, or marriage, it will either reap fruitful or frightful results.

Make sure the people who step into your life, have something to add to it and vice versa.

I'm a living witness, relationships are much like your credit union or banking service. If you keep letting people make more withdrawals, than deposits in your life, you will end up bankrupt. You have to get to a place in your life that says, "If you can't add and multiply in my life, then don't waste my time by subtracting and dividing my resources." Your current relationships are like currency. Are they enriching you or depleting you?

I'm convinced that some people should have had a starring role, in the movie *Takers*, simply because they lack the capacity to give. If you don't want your existence to make a difference, then be a taker. However, if you want to be remembered, then be a giver.

THIS LITTLE LIGHT OF MINE

Have you ever compared a lit candle to an unlit one? Right, one has a flame the other doesn't. What does a candle lose that is lit, by illuminating an unlit candle? Exactly, nothing! A candle that lights an unlit candle never loses its flame, it remains ignited.

The same works true in the literal sense, giving to somebody else never diminishes your value, it just adds to it. Acts 20:35 affirms, "For it is better to give, than to receive." Yet the thing about giving, is that you can't help but to receive when you give.

The greatest receiver, is the one who knows how to be a giver. Each day make it a point, to light and ignite somebody's life. You never lose anything by it, you gain everything because of it. The more that you ignite others, the greater your faith, focus, and flame will remain.

Pack your bags and leave all of the negative people in your past, because they don't fit into your future. Much like social media, some people you need to unfriend, unfollow, delete, and others you just need to block from going in and out of your life. It's time to do some cleaning and sweep all of the negative people, out of your life.

UNHEALTHY RELATIONSHIPS

Realize that toxic relationships, are a biohazard to your breakthrough and purpose. Toxic connections and relationships are unhealthy, which will in turn destroy your life. Toxic relationships will not only cause you heartbreak and heartache, but heartburn and heart attack.

They say, "It's not what you walk away from, it's what you walk away with." Many of us have walked away from toxic relationships, but we have walked away with a broken heart, emotional baggage, scars of abuse, mistrust, depression, addiction, and low self-esteem. These were not parting gifts, but curses that will destroy your life and the generations to come. Give yourself the gift of healing and forgiveness, to break the curse of bitterness and brokenness. Forgive whoever hurt you and forgive yourself, for allowing it to happen. You will never be better, if you continue to remain bitter. Loose it and let it go!

You don't need a whole bunch of people in your life, you just need the right people. The right people and relationships won't reduce you, they will produce greater purpose in you. Never reduce yourself, to fit in with people who don't like you anyway. The people who try to reduce you, can see in you what you don't see in yourself. They can see your purpose and potential. As a result, they will try to destroy you, so that you don't walk in your God-given greatness. When God is for you, the who doesn't matter. When God favors you, people who don't like you, can't do anything about it. Be cognizant of who is in your circle. Major dreamers, don't associate with dream killers and minor thinkers.

GIFTED FOR GREATNESS

Recognize that your haters are your elevators and they don't like you, because you're gifted. Realize that if you're gifted, you will be afflicted. The enemy only attacks people who are gifted. The enemy can't destroy your gift, but if he can stop and destroy you, then you won't use the gift that God gave you. Since you're gifted, you will be lifted.

Pablo Picasso is world renowned, for his gift as a painter. He influenced modern art, with many of his cubist style/abstract paintings such as, *The Reservoir, Horta de Ebro*. Picasso declared, "The meaning of life is to find your gift, but the purpose of life is to give your gift away." Picasso did it with a paintbrush, I do it with a mic and a pen. How do you use your gift? By all means, don't stop using your gift. Stir it up, cultivate it, and work your gift from within.

They say, "A job is what you're paid for, your calling is what you're made for." Your calling is connected to your gifting. If you do the preparing, God will do the directing. Proverbs 18:16, "A gift opens the way and ushers the giver, into the presence of the great." (Discover powerful principles, on how to use your gift, in my book, *Unwrap The Gift In YOU!*).

IT'S TIME TO DELIVER

An old rap song said, "When I move, you move…just like that." Much like that same verse, that's how God operates. When He begins to move in your spirit, you must follow His vision, purpose, plans, and preparations that He has impregnated in your life. You are pregnant with purpose, promise, possibility, and potential.

This is your time, to give birth to everything within you. Overcome your past, in order to embrace the opportunities and endless possibilities of your future.

I'm convinced that opportunity has a favorite song and that is, "On to the next one." If you don't do anything with the gifts, talents, intelligence, and creativity that is within you, opportunities will pass you by. They say, "Opportunity is often overlooked by people, because it's dressed in overalls and looks like work." Opportunity may not always come in the form, that you're looking for, but you must be receptive enough to take advantage of it.

OVERCOME THE INNER-ME

It's time to stop being your own worst enemy, it's time to become your best friend. For some of us, the greatest enemy can be the inner-me, because of a negative concept of self, which keeps us in a state of regression, rather than progression. A positive state of mind, will usher us into the spectrum of success. Shut the door, draw a line in the sand, and announce that you will not be a liability any longer, your life will be an asset to somebody...even if the somebody is you!

Don't go negative on the negative, stay positive in the negative...breakthrough is on the way! Let's be real, yes we have been victims, but we have also been perpetrators. As long as this world revolves and spins around, what goes around will come back around.

WHAT YOU SOW, WILL GROW

What you sow, you will reap. Your harvest is just an indication, of the seeds that you've planted. Begin to plant seeds of strength, sagacity, and superabundant power. You may be going through, but you're coming out stronger than when you went in. You're not just going to go through, but you're going to grow through every circumstance and situation.

None of us are perfect, but it doesn't mean we should stop striving to attain perfection. We all deal with a myriad of issues. We have our own idiosyncratic behaviors and personal proclivities. In order to cancel your subscription to the past and everything that draws you away, from your purpose, you have to cast your cares on God and place it in His hands. Your hands are too small to handle it, God's hands are big enough to deal with it.

LET'S PLAY CATCH

Your subscription to the past won't be canceled, until you cast your cares on the one, who cares for you. Don't cast your cares on Facebook, Instagram, Twitter, or the phone…take your issues to God's throne. I like what God does because He looks at your issues and says, "Lets play catch."

God is saying, "Throw your issues my way and I'll throw you inspiration. Throw me your pain and I'll throw you power. Throw me your depression and I'll throw you joy." Whatever you give to God, He will exchange it for your benefit. I personally know, that when you give Him your sickness, He will give you healing. If you give Him your broken heart, He will repair and restore it. As my little brother Elijah would say, "When God heals you, don't pick at the wound."

Don't make the mistake, of taking your focus off God, because you will drop the ball. If you allow other people to distract you, then you will drop the blessing that God has for you. Stay focused and keep your eyes on the prize. In the game of life, God is like a relief pitcher, so that you can experience victory instead of defeat. He will strikeout and shutout your opposition.

THINK VICTORY

Choose victory despite how you feel. You have made choices out of weakness long enough, it's time to choose from strength. Win the mental battle, because there is a battle for your mind.

II Corinthians 10:4 affirms, "For the weapons of our warfare are not carnal, but mighty through God to the pulling down of strongholds." In order to overcome the obstacles and battles of life, you've got to be transformed by thoughts of power and peace.

When you're transformed, you won't be conformed to your situation. God wants you to use the cognitive energy of your mind and the sagacity within your spirit, to operate out of faith for victory. The enemy wants to control your mind through fear, to be defeated.

FAITH VS. FEAR

Breaking news! You can't doubt and have faith, at the same time. Simply because, one will cancel out the other. Fear paralyzes you, but only faith mobilizes you. You can't unlock the door of faith, until you shut the door of fear.

You can live in **FEAR**, to *Face Everything And Run* or walk by **FAITH**, to *Face Everything And Rise*! You won't run in fear, if you walk by faith! How you think about your situation, will determine 3 things:

1. Whether you stay in it.

2. Die while experiencing it.

3. Live through dying places and emerge victorious because of it.

Faith is the catalyst, that will propel you towards victory. Proverbs 3:5 reminds us, that if you lean to your own understanding, you will fall. However, if you trust God, then He will direct your paths. I'm not trying to preach to you, I'm just empowering you through principles that I have learned. You must trust God to see you through, when you can't see your way out.

For too long, you have subscribed to what everybody else said about you…what you would never become, or overcome. It goes like this: "Nobody ever graduated from college, nobody is a millionaire in our family, mama got pregnant at 16, grandmother got pregnant at 17, so it's bound to happen to you." If nobody has ever done the impossible, you're the best one to do it. You are that special somebody! Break the negative cycle!

WHAT'S THE FORECAST?

When negative people have stormy situations in their life, all of a sudden they become a meteorologist and try to forecast your future. Come rain, sleet, hail (hell), or snow, you can make it through the rough terrains of life. Despite the overcast, I can see the radiance of the sun breaking through the clouds in your life. A cloudy day, is no match for a sunny disposition.

Don't ascribe or subscribe, to a negative forecast about your future. Don't allow failure, to frame the picture of your life. Begin to believe that the picture of your past will not permeate your future. You're not breaking down, you're breaking through. You're breaking out of the box, to become better than you've ever been.

When everybody else is looking at your past, God is looking at your heart. The right people in your life, will look beyond what you've done and see you for who you can become. They will look past the person, that you've been and begin to see you for who you will be.

It's interesting that people don't have a law degree, but still want to judge you. Let them judge you, they will never see what God sees, when He looks at you. What God has for you, is greater than any barrier that anyone could use to stop you. If God is for you, it doesn't matter the who that's against you, (Romans 8:31).

DECLARATION OF INDEPENDENCE

The sad reality is that people want to perpetuate a false sense of perfection, and in the process they lose their authenticity. I am not perfect, but I am genuine. Can we be candid? It's just you and me talking. Everybody has issues, from the person reading this book, to the one who wrote the book. Identifying them does not make you weak, a refusal to acknowledge them does.

Stop living in the specter of your past. Give your past a funeral, because it's already dead. Make a decree, your personal Declaration of Independence to cancel your subscription, because you're through with these issues. We hold these truths to be self-evident…that all men/women have issues. However, we are not the sum of what we have done. We can experience life, liberty, love and laughter, on a new level. What we can become, is greater than what we have done.

Cancel your subscription to issues of heartbreak, issues of rejection, issues of abuse, issues of insecurity, issues of low self-esteem, issues of abandonment, issues of toxic relationships, issues of financial instability, and issues of a lack of self-love. Despite our finite frailties, God has healing tissues for our hurting issues.

I PLEDGE ALLEGIANCE

Make a personal pledge of allegiance. A pledge is a solemn promise and commitment, that one makes, through words to honor that vow. Make this personal pledge with me, by placing your right hand over your heart.

Believe it as you say it:

I pledge to love myself.

I pledge to see the value in myself and others.

I pledge to walk in purpose.

I pledge to walk in healing and forgiveness.

I pledge to be the best that I was made to be.

I pledge to honor God with my life.

I pledge to make a difference each day.

I pledge to heal my heart.

I pledge to walk in love, victory, and purpose.

Do more than say it, begin to live it each day.

YOUR SUBSCRIPTION IS CANCELED

The pledge you just spoke, broke the nagging negativity

over your life! Beyond a subscription, many of us have had

a personal membership to mediocrity, madness, and mess.

Cancel your subscription to sickness, you're healed.

Cancel your subscription to depression, you've got joy.

Cancer is canceled. Not just a physical cancer, but a mental and spiritual cancer. The things that have devoured your deliverance, destiny, and determination.

Situations in life have been eating away at your joy, hope, and peace of mind. Dreams have been afflicted and infected with a virus of victimization, but God's Word will transform you until you become affected by victory! Your situation is not too dead. God can't resurrect you out of it!

ACCESS DENIED

Yes, you may be alone but you're not lonely. In times of isolation and separation, God will give you revelation to make you one with Him. Overcome loneliness and procrastination. When people, situations, and negative thoughts come your way, just say, "Access denied." If you give negativity an inch, it will take a mile.

Deny toxic relationships access into your life. You are not an entrance and exit gateway, stop allowing people to walk in and out of your life. Start telling them, "Access denied!" Don't allow anything to upset the flow of your joy. Move beyond your past and embrace your future. Tell yourself, "I'm through with this mess, so I can accept God's best."

ACCESS GRANTED

Do more than exist and begin to live, with purpose, on purpose, and for a purpose because you have a dynamic purpose. Don't let negativity become your reality. Live, laugh, and love again! You have life, faith, vision, hope, peace, purpose, resilience, and persevering power. It's in you, it's in there!

Access the greatness within you and give birth to it. You're pregnant with purpose. Don't abort your vision, your future, or your destiny. Deliver and birth it. Cancel your subscription, to every negative issue. It's over, let it go. You can't change the past, but you can presently shape your future, because you've got love under new management.

CHAPTER 3

Love Under New Management

A few years ago, actor and director, Tyler Perry brought to the silver screen, *Why Did I Get Married?* This particular movie, unveiled the ups and downs in love, life, and relationships, within the matrix of marriage.

Researches suggest, that more than 50% of all marriages end in divorce. Indeed the institution of marriage is under attack and in the crosshairs of our country. As a caveat, the divorce rate is higher in the church, than it is among the secular culture. Some may say, "If folks who are Bible-toting believers can't keep it together, then why would the folks in the world, want to walk down the aisle?"

WHY WOULD I GET MARRIED?

The issues of marriage and divorce may even make Tyler Perry himself, think of writing another movie, *Why Would I Get Married?* I say it sarcastically, yet seriously because of an alarming study about dating, relationships, and marriage in recent years. According to a Pew Research study, "40% of Americans, say there is no need for marriage." What are your thoughts on these findings?

It seems as if there is a growing sub-culture of individuals who are choosing to be single, for life, by "Abstaining from marriage." Some of the reasons given were those who would rather cohabit (as my grandmother would call it, "Shacking up"), engage in long-term dating, some see it more financially feasible, bad relationship experiences, etc. Are these valid reasons, to not walk down the aisle? What if you didn't grow up in a household with a strong marriage example, could that impact your decision to marry or not?

Such is the dynamic in the black community, where according to LifeSiteNews.com, 54% of homes are fatherless. I grew up in a divorced home, being raised by my mother. Without a doubt, divorce or an absentee parent, will shape any persons view of relationships, which can be juxtaposed ambivalently and optimistically.

PARENTS JUST DON'T UNDERSTAND

Back in the day I was a big fan of, the television sitcom, *The Fresh Prince of Bel-Air*. I'm telling you, I didn't miss an episode of Will Smith and Carlton's (Alfonso Ribeiro) comedic bantering. Don't laugh, but I still know the theme song to this day (and you probably do to). Yes, I was that kid with a high-top fade, rockin' Air Jordan sneakers, who loved sports, music, and video games.

All I wanted to do, was collect sports cards, watch TV, go to the movies, play basketball, and use Will Smith's pick-up lines (that I learned from the show) on the cutest girl at school. Mr. Smith is a big movie star now, but during the late 80s/early 90s, he was honing his chops as an actor and rapper. During that time, DJ Jazzy Jeff and The Fresh Prince (Will Smith), released a hit song, *Parents Just Don't Understand.*

The rap song highlighted that parents don't understand the fashion, lifestyle, or "cool" world of youth culture, albeit they were once young too. If you have seen the video or heard the song, you can assert that, The Fresh Prince was quite mischievous. Yet, in still his parents were strict and firm with him, time and time again.

Does the modern day parent understand, the importance and value of time in their child's life?

In a span of 24 hours, family researchers suggest that "The average father (who lives in the home), only has 7 minutes of interaction, with his son/daughter. The average mother spends approximately, 34 minutes a day with her son/daughter." Who is spending the most time with our children, if it's not the parents?

RAISED BY JEEZY AND JAY-Z

Believe it or not, many of the young people that I mentor and teach, are raising themselves. To witness the hurt, pain, and lack of love in the lives of our youth, is heartbreaking. Kids are raising themselves on a daily diet of *BET, MTV,* and *PlayStation 3*. It seems as if the parental voice, has been silenced and substituted, by celebrities such as Nicki Minaj, Beyoncé, Miley Cyrus, Young Jeezy, and Jay-Z.

IT'S LOVE O'CLOCK

Some parents just don't understand, that the value of time in a child's life, is more significant than the money spent to provide them with the best life. However, to a child, love is spelled…T-I-M-E!

I'm grateful to have a mother who raised me and expressed her love to me, by spending time to instill values within me. There are still good parents in this world, who are proactive in there children's lives. I want to applaud all of them, especially if you are that kind of parent. I like to say, "It's Love O'Clock…TIME to show love to somebody."

A HOUSE IS NOT A HOME

Without a doubt, as we look around our communities, we can see that we are a generation of fatherless sons and daddyless daughters. Our families are broken. As the iconic vocalist, Luther Vandross suggested, "Just because it's a house, doesn't mean it's a home." The stark difference between a house and a home, is the lack or provision of love.

The idea of love has become some foreign, alien, and mystical word to many of us in a number of ways. To a certain degree, it's as if you reach for it but you can't grasp it. For many of us, love has either never been experienced, it required us to give up something, or it was connected to a lot of pain. If it was promulgated toward you in that way, it wasn't real love.

LOVE LIFTED ME

Real love doesn't tear you down, it lifts you up. Due to the experiences that we've had, some of us have become so numb to pain, that it hurts to love and be happy. I wonder have you ever been there? I know people who have had negative experiences in relationships, that say, "If things are going right, then something must be wrong." Sadly they live their life with a guard up, suspicious of any and everybody, because they've been hurt.

FACTS VS. TRUTH

The father of psychoanalysis, Sigmund Freud suggested, "The reason we are the way we are as adults, is directly connected to who we were as children and the experiences we've had." Freud is expressing to us, that we can be no better than our childhood development, due to what we have been exposed to.

A noted psychologist, Francis Galton, coined the phrase and developed the concept of *Nature vs. Nurture.* The abstract idea is steeped in the fact that it's not always who we are, but how we have been raised; our environments, and interactions, which play a significant factor in our lives.

The substratum of *Nature,* underscores the fact that genetics and natural influences, shape one's behavior and decision making. On the other end, *Nurture* argues that a person develops through the influences of people, experiences, and interactions to formulate one's life. In essence, is the sum total of who you are innate, or is it learned through experience?

I'm a living witness, that you can have the facts and still not have the truth. The fact is that your past impacts your life. The truth is that, you are not your past and the sum of your experiences. Your situation does not define you, unless you allow it to. Yes, you may have been hurt, but you can begin to heal and experience the power of love, despite the pain.

You may say, "All I have experienced was hurt, pain, mistrust, and unhappiness, so how can I embrace love from God? Will He let me down, like everybody else? How can I embrace, what I have never experienced?" Many times we bag, box, and bring our baggage into various relationships. However, they never become fruitful because we have not rid ourselves, of the vestiges of our past.

GOING IN CIRCLES

Yes, you're delivered but you haven't healed. What I mean is that, you're no longer in the situation that brought pain, but your mind and heart are still battling with it. Physically you may be free, but psychologically, spiritually, and relationally there is brokenness within. Healing is not an overnight instance, it's a continual process. When you begin to trust God and experience His love, there will be healing that flows through your life. God will show you how to love yourself and as a result, love others.

If you live your life going in circles, you will never make substantial progress. You must use every breaking point, to break free from the circumstances that seek to break you down. Break free from the whirlwind of worry and the tornado of trials and tribulations. When you begin to break the cycle, you will experience love under new management.

OUT WITH THE OLD, IN WITH THE NEW

The old mindset and lifestyle, will be replaced by a new level of thinking and living. Your mind is like a computer that stores information and can be used as a resource, to connect to your world. You can't run new software on an old computer, just like you can't use new ideas on an old mindset.

What is on your mental hard drive and what are you downloading into your mind? You can't live positively, if you're thinking negatively. The laws of sowing and reaping, have always been true and that is you can't plant orange seeds and reap apples. The same is true in life, what you sow will grow. The seeds that you plant on the inside, will manifest into trees of truth or weeds of worry, on the outside.

God is the conduit, by which love under new management is experienced. There is unity but also a deep divide, between God's love and His law, the cross and the commandments, religion and relationship. Law denotes, if you break the commandment you die. On the contrary, love affirms that you broke the commandment. However, despite your weakness, God's grace is sufficient (2 Corinthians 12:9).

Grace is the bridge, that merges God's law and His love. So if I am out of fellowship, our love relationship can and will be restored. You're not so far gone, that His love can't pull you back. Religion says, "If I obey, God will love me." Relationship says, "Because God loves me, I can obey." John 4:24 declares, "For God is a Spirit and they that worship Him, must worship Him in spirit and in truth." There is no way, that you can revere and worship, what you don't love. You can't worship in truth, if you're living a lie.

There are distinctive differences, between the Old and New Testament. One is that the Old Testament, places an emphasis on the fear or reverence of God. On the other hand, the New Testament emphasizes the love of God. If you have experienced God's love and it lives within you, it becomes the air you breathe. His love becomes the ebb and flow of life, expressed in your relationships.

U AND I

Let's look at the matrix of relationships. For any relationship to flourish, there must be communication. There is no way that you can spell *communication*, without *"u"* and *"i"*. It takes a committed tandem and teamwork to communicate. The building block of communication, is the foundational framework, for the development of that relationship. Whether in business, dating, or marriage, good communication is necessary.

A lack of communication can suffocate a relationship, but good communication can breathe life into it. One of the biggest communication mistakes we make, is when we listen to reply, instead of listening to understand. Listening is not, waiting to talk!

As men and women communicate, we need to understand that the essence of communication is not solely about your ability to speak, it's more importantly about your ability to listen. It's not only about what you say, it's how you listen to what is being said. Communication and comprehension, are essential components to relational compatibility.

LIFE ON MARS AND VENUS

Growing up I would hear people say, "Men are from Mars and women are from Venus." This statement meant that men and women, don't understand each other and they are literally from two different planets. Yes, it may feel that way at times, but the benefits outweigh the frustrations. Maybe a better description, is that men are like waffles and women are like spaghetti.

Here's what I mean, as men we have our categories for things, and we generally don't intertwine everything together. We will compartmentalize things and often separate facts from feelings. Women have a propensity to mix, intertwine, and merge things together.

For instance, ask a woman how was her day today, go ahead ask. I guarantee, she will tell you how it was from 6:32 a.m., when she awoke and put her feet in her slippers, to the time at 11:09 p.m., that she wrapped her hair for the night. Her explanation will be descriptive and in the details, she will express her feelings about the occurrences of the day. Indeed there is truth in humor.

On the other hand, ask a man how was his day and generally he will say, "It was good." Now some men, may give you a little more than that, often from questions raised. In all sincerity though, for him it was a good day.

The facts about his day, will generally be conveyed, more than his feelings during the day.

A woman will express, how she felt and render the details. A man is going to give you, the facts and figures. Just because men and women are different, doesn't mean that a specific gender is deficient. Both men and women, are communicative beings. We just express ourselves differently, via verbal and nonverbal methods of communication.

HOW MUCH IS IN YOUR BANK?

On this topic of communication, everybody has a daily word bank, whether you know it or not. Communication researchers suggest that "Men on average use 10,000 words a day (5,000 words at their place of employment). Women use approximately 20,000 words each day (10,000 words at their place of employment)." Let's analyze this word bank. When a husband and wife leave their respective jobs/careers and come home, there is a mathematical gap in communication.

For instance, they each arrive at home, in their "His and hers *Mercedes Benz*" and take time to relax. In doing so, now the conversation begins about the day and their relationship. So the man uses his remaining 5,000 words, during the conversation (keep in mind, that he's now depleted his word bank) and the woman has another 10,000 words, still left in her bank.

So think about it, now the man is out of conversation and the woman is still communicating. Have you ever experienced this? If so, what side were you on in the conversation? Now she's saying to him, "Why don't you talk to me?" He's thinking, "I don't have anything to say" (little does she know, that he used up all of the words in his bank).

Now brothers if she says to you, "Why am I the only one talking?" I guess you can tell her, "I've used all of the words, in my bank for the day!" Ladies I'm sure you're thinking, "Well if he's smart, he will borrow words from my bank, find some on credit, and keep the conversation going" (3 snaps and a neck roll included). As funny as it sounds, oftentimes men and women clash, because of communication differences or simply the lack of understanding one another.

LISTEN AND SILENT

For any relationship to have success, you have to talk, but you also have to listen. Both are intertwined in the art of communication. I believe that women, are the stronger communicative beings. The ability to communicate can be an asset, as opposed to a liability when used carefully.

Do you have the composure to listen and hear, beyond what your eyes can only see? Don't just listen to what people are saying, listen to what they are not saying. It takes discipline to listen and be silent. It's interesting that the words, "Listen and silent" have the same letters, yet both are priceless words. Our words are like swords that can chop somebody, or sharpen them. We must use them wisely, as we communicate daily.

The immersion of communication and feelings, is what makes women highly resourceful and compassionate nurturers. On many occasions, when I was a child, I witnessed my mother create something out of nothing. Many women today, also possess the creativity to do the same.

IT'S A DIFFERENT WORLD

You don't need Dwayne Wayne and Whitley Gilbert, the star characters, of the hit TV show *A Different World* to tell you, that we're living in a different world. Just look around, you can see it, these are the signs of the times. Back in the day, people would make a point to get to know you, before they got to "Know you" if you know what I'm saying.

Love, lust, and like have been abused and misused countlessly. Oftentimes, we make the mistake of confusing the three. It generally happens when you look for love externally, before developing it internally. When you become a person of love, you will begin to attract real love that's selfless…not lust, that's selfish.

Many of our hearts have been broken and bankrupt, by people who mishandled love. As a result we have emotionally, psychologically, and relationally filed for love

bankruptcy. Yet, I Corinthians 13 spells out the blueprint

for love's bountifulness.

THE LOVE LETTER

The Corinthian letter suggests that "Love is patient, love is

kind. Love does not envy or keep a record of wrongs." The

passage affirms, that you can be intoxicated with the

exuberance of your intellectual verbosity, to where you

speak with royal eloquence and angelic ecstasy.

Yet, if you're a hateful, bitter, mean, and ruthless

person it means nothing. In essence, you simply sound like

the irritating noise of a rusty gate, or a squeaky door in

need of WD-40. Only the oil of God's anointing, can flush

out anger, bitterness, and strife in your life. When love

flows through your heart, you're quick to forgive and slow

to criticize. When you express that you love something or someone, what does that mean? How do you define love? In relationships, it's worth asking, "Do I love you the way I love or do I love you, the way that you desire for me to love you?"

There are a plethora of expressions and interpretations for love. The English linguistic interpretation to define love, is very limited and narrow in its approach. For instance you can say, "I love that dress, I love my dog, I love my husband, I love my wife" and there be no exact definition to distinguish the meaning, because it's limited within the scope of its interpretation.

In examination of the word *Heart,* the transliterated term is from the Hebrew lexicon, *Leb*. The term *Leb* is defined as spirit, mind, will, heart (as moral character), and the seat of one's desires. The *Leb* is the engine for life and the driving force for love. The Ancient Greeks took it a step further and analyzed *Love* in 4 dimensions, from a panoramic perspective using the words: *Eros, Philia, Storge,* and *Agape.* I know you're saying, "So what does each word mean?" I'm so glad that you asked.

Eros is passionate love, with sensual desire and longing. The modern Greek word, "Erotas" means intimate love.

Philia means friendship or affectionate love. It includes loyalty to family, friends, and community. It's also rooted, in the etymological name of the city of Philadelphia, which means "Brotherly love."

Storge is natural affection, like that felt by parents for their children. The Greeks used Storge to describe relationships within the family.

God doesn't operate in *Eros, Philia,* or *Storge,* He operates in *Agape.* The terms *Eros, Phila,* and *Storge* describe love with limits. However, *Agape* has no limitations because it denotes unconditional love. *Agape* is love without limits and the deepest form of love. *Agape* is used in the biblical passage, known as the *Love letter* in I Corinthians 13, being described as sacrificial love.

LOVE WITHOUT LIMITS?

As a human being with limitations and frailties, can you love someone unconditionally? Think about that for a minute. Do you have the capacity, to love without limits and conditions? I would suggest, emphatically no!

The Bible never commanded us to love unconditionally, because God knows that we are finite and flawed. However, He commands us to exemplify and express love to each other, even through our flawed mechanics.

Every relationship has a deal breaker, if it's not communicated and expressed, it is thought about. Somethings you can tolerate, but other things are intolerable. The only one, who can love without limits and express love unconditionally, is God.

You and I, are too flawed to love unconditionally. You can have the intent to love, but it must entail the extent, that goes beyond finite limitations. The more connected we are to God, the more His love is able to flow through us. As a result, we can look beyond the conditions of others, to embrace their needs. If God looked beyond your faults and saw your needs, then surely you can do the same for someone else.

THE ULTIMATE GIFT

A lot of times, we give gifts to express our love or engender someone's interest in us. Eventually the gifts get old, break, and fade into a distant memory. I've come to the realization that love is the only gift, that you can keep giving and never run out of it. Love is the ultimate gift, that keeps on giving. Tangible gifts don't replace love, because love is the greatest gift. You may be alone, but it doesn't mean that you have to be lonely. God has never left you and He placed love, within your heart. You can never expect anybody to love you, until you start loving yourself.

Eugene Peterson said, "The person who refuses to love, doesn't know the first thing about God, because God is love. You can't know Him, if you don't love." In essence, I can't love God, if I don't know God and I can't know God, if I don't love Him. When you know His love for you, it makes you love Him back and show love to somebody else. Knowing God's love, gives you self-love and self-love births a love for others.

God's love, His Agape is so high that you can't climb over it, so wide that you can't go around it, and it's rooted so deep that you can't go under it. He just wants you to walk through it. You can't be worse than His best, you can't be more evil than His goodness, and you can't hate more than He loves. God's love is like GPS, He finds us in our mess and makes our destination a great message. Only God can find you, where everybody else left you.

LOVE LESSON

Love does not restrict or inhibit, it releases. Love doesn't mean, put a LoJack on somebody. Love doesn't call you every 5 minutes, wondering where you are, or calculating how long it takes you to get from the grocery store to the house. Realize that's not love, that's control.

Love doesn't restrain you, love constrains you. If love is a restraint that means it desires to control the object. When love is a constraint, it seeks to be the subject in control of one's self. Real love does not confine you, it refines you.

RULES FOR RELATIONSHIPS

Love under new management, is about more than keeping a bunch of rules, it's about relationship. If it was only about rules, God would have thrown you away a long time ago. Yet His grace, mercy, and love for you said, "Don't run from me, run to me." When you run to Him, He will restore you back into relationship.

You can't keep the rules without a relationship, but He will love you until you love Him back. Your love for

Him, will cause you to keep the rules. Jesus declared in John 14:15, "If you love me, keep my commandments."

When you connect to God, it's love under new management. If they tell you that they love you and treat you like trash, I guarantee their lips are lying. I can hear what you're saying, but your actions are screaming.

IS IT LOVE OR LIP SERVICE?

Don't say one thing and do another. Get those Jekyll and Hyde folks, out of your life. You don't need phony, fair-weather friends, and fickle folks in your life. Depending on how somebody treats you, is an indication of who they are and what you allow.

You give people a blueprint on how to treat you, by the way that you treat yourself. Teach people how to treat you. The substratum of how they treat you, is also an indication of how they think about themselves. If they don't think much of themselves, they won't think much of you and as a result, will treat you less than you deserve.

If they really love you and love themselves, then they will know how to treat you in the process. Their actions will show you, better than their words can tell you. Their actions will let you know, if it's real love or lip service. Love is expressed in how they treat you, not just what they say to you. Indeed love is a verb, it requires action. Don't just say it, show it!

Don't believe what they say, at the expense of ignoring what you see. Love is action and it will show through, in how they treat you. Words fall on deaf ears, when actions are seen with wide eyes! Realize that love doesn't tear you down, it lifts you up. When it's real love, you won't have to question, the answers will show in their actions. Love goes beyond what's said, it's shown.

The right one will recognize, that you are a red box and a gold bow…a gift to the world. If they don't recognize your value, that's their loss. Never lose sight of your value! You are a gift!

THE ROOT OF YOUR FRUIT

A lot of people want the gifts of the Spirit (I Corinthians 12:8-10), but don't have the fruit of the Spirit (Galatians 5:22, 23). I'm talking about "Love, joy, peace, longsuffering, gentleness, goodness, faith, meekness, and temperance."

You won't have the gifts, without the fruits. The spiritual gift is directly connected to the fruit, but your fruit is an indication of your root. The seeds that you're sowing, are directly connected to the fruit that you're bearing. What are you planted and rooted in? Is your spirit rooted in bitterness, lust, depression, anger, malice, confusion, etc? If so, then the fruit of your results, will be a byproduct of the root of your actions.

Your fruit is only an indication of your root. Psalm 1:3, "And he shall be like a tree planted by the rivers of water, that bringeth forth his fruit in his season; his leaf also shall not wither and whatsoever he doeth shall prosper."

You can't walk in hate and expect to live a life of love. The spectrum of fear and love are contradistinctive, because "Perfect love casteth out fear" (I John 4:18). Scripture declares in 2 Timothy 1:7, "For God hath not given us the spirit of fear; but of power, and of love, and of a sound mind."

FEAR PARALYZES, FAITH MOBILIZES

You can't have a sound mind and walk in the power of love, if your spirit is rooted in fear. If you abide in Him, as His words abide in you (John 15:7), then you won't run in fear, you will walk by faith. You can't walk by faith, if you're paralyzed fear. It is fear that will paralyze you, but only faith will mobilize you.

EXERCISE YOUR FAITH

God does not operate in fear and neither should you. Hebrews 11:6, "But without faith, it is impossible to please God." You can't let your faith atrophy, or fear will be strongest in your life. Your faith is like a muscle, that strengthens when you stretch it. The more you exercise your faith, the stronger it will become. It must be stretched and exercised.

Hebrews 11:1, "Now faith is the substance of things hoped for, the evidence of things not seen." I don't know about you, but I need substance in my life, I need an anchor, I need a sure foundation, and I need love under new management.

Don't let somebody's mismanagement of love, stop you from believing in love. Don't let disappointments stop you, from believing in love and receiving love. The right person will make you realize, why the wrong one never worked in the first place. Be patient, the right one is coming. There's a difference between, "The right one and the one right now." Don't get in such a hurry, that you settle for less, than God's best for your life.

HERE WE GROW AGAIN

The more I love God, the more I trust Him. Real faith is the kind, that's been hell tested and God approved. You've got to not only go through something, you've got to GROW through something. Love stimulates faith in God. Galatians 5:6, "For faith worketh by love." Love doesn't neglect, it protects. Love is not selfish, it's selfless.

You can give without loving, but you cannot love without giving. John 3:16, "For God so loved the world, that He gave his only begotten Son." To give of oneself is the ultimate sign of love for God, others, and self. When you starting learning, healing, and loving, then you will start growing.

BLAST PAST YOUR PAST

The sad reality is that too many of us, are presently living in the past. You can't marry your future, until you divorce your past. There is no denying the fact, that everybody has a past. How much of someone's past, is too much to bring into your future?

Realize that love is not about finding a perfect person, it's about learning to love an imperfect person. Love is not a taker, love is a giver. Love understands that it's not about what you have, it's about who you are, and whose you are. Recognize that you are God's child and you are deserving of love. You can't be bought or sold, you're priceless. Gifts don't replace love, for love is the greatest gift. When you look through the lens of love beyond someone's past, then you will see that it's about their heart, not the way they start.

HEAL BEFORE YOU DEAL

My mother, Dr. Janice K. Connor, was speaking at a recent conference on inner-healing, forgiveness, and purpose. She told the people, that "Healing begins in the heart, when one is ready to dissect the root cause." While she was speaking, I meditated on her aphorism and made connections to my life.

There are certain words and statements that hit home to your heart, in order to heal you before you deal with someone new. You can't show love, with bitterness and hatred in your heart. Let love, heal your heart and mend every wound.

Some people hate the truth and fall in love with a lie. God will love you with the evidence, when people will hate you based on speculation. Dr. Martin Luther King, Jr. said, "Hate cannot drive out hate, only love can do that."

Be too busy showing love, to hate somebody else. You can't love anybody, if you don't love yourself first.

THE NEW LANGUAGE

For many of our youth today, they are living in a generation where loyalty is nothing more than a tattoo, lying is the new truth, and love is a foreign language. It's foreign because LOVE has sadly been defined as, "Legs Open Very Easily."

We are not living in The Victorian Era, of sexual restraint and morality. Our culture has become overtly sexualized, to where lust is the new language. Understand that love doesn't play games with you. It doesn't seek to take or perpetuate negativity upon you. Love doesn't pawn or pimp you. Love doesn't bring confusion, it brings clarity. Lust and like won't lead you to love, only God's love letter will do that.

YOU'VE GOT MAIL

God has given you a love letter. Open His word document and you will find peace, love, joy, comfort, hope, sagacity, and strength. God loves you just the way that you are and He loves you too much, to let you stay the way that you are.

Indeed, true love accepts you the way you are, but it won't leave you the way you are. Love doesn't leave you where you are, it lifts you to where you need to be. Just like the song expresses, "Love lifted me, love lifted me... when nothing else could help, love lifted me."

WHAT'S LOVE GOT TO DO WITH IT?

You can't express, what you don't possess. When love fills your heart, there's no space for hate. Love is strong enough to find peace, from broken pieces. So what's love got to do with it? Everything! Romans 8:38 persuades us to know that love is too strong for death to outlast it, too extensive for life to outlive it, too majestic for angels, principalities, and powers to dominate it.

Love is too far beyond, for the present or the future to blockade it, and too high/wide to get around it. Through it all, "I'll let nothing separate me from the love of God, which is in Christ Jesus our Lord" (Romans 8:39).

ONLY LOVE CAN DO IT

Never forget that only love, can turn stumbling blocks into stepping stones. Only love can transform death into life. Love can help a hurting hater. Love can be good to somebody, who was never good to you.

If I was an English teacher, I would tell you that love is a verb, because it requires your action. If I was a Math teacher, I would inform you that the answer to love's equation, is "3 nails + 1 cross = 4 given." God decided to give love, because it has inexhaustible power.

Let's be an example of love according to the *Love letter* in I Corinthians 13, which declares, "Love is patient, love is kind, love is never jealous, and love is not envious." When we understand the power of love and God's love, then we can love ourselves and express love to each other.

YOU BETTER RECOGNIZE

When you connect to God, He provides you with love under new management. No games, gimmicks, tricks, or schemes. It's His love for you out of the depth of who He is, that empowers you to love yourself, love others, and walk in your unique purpose.

His love for you reconciles you to Him, yourself, and to those around you. Love has a boomerang effect. The more love that you share with others, the more it comes back to you.

Love is more than just a word and it intensifies, when we give it meaning. Love is not about what it says, love is about what it does.

LOVE THROUGH A NEW LENS

See love through a different lens. Take time to meditate and recognize the attributes of love:

Love never gives up.

Love cares more for others than self.

Love doesn't want what it doesn't have.

Love doesn't strut. Love isn't puffed up.

Love is selfless, not selfish.

Love doesn't keep score of sins.

Love doesn't revel in seeking revenge.

Love takes pleasure in truth. Love always looks for the best, not the worst. Love never looks back, its always looking forward. Love keeps going to the end. Love lifted you and me.

CHAPTER 4

Take Off The Mask

Is today's culture and society, all about superficiality? Some would argue, that we are living in such times. Simply because, many people would rather look successful, than actually put in the work to be successful.

Many would rather flaunt with a façade of smiling on the outside, yet in reality they are depressed and discombobulated on the inside. Truth be told, we often hide behind what we possess on the outside, to cover up what we're void of on the inside.

I NEED A MAKEOVER

If you're anticipating this chapter to be about beauty secrets, or the top ten ways to keep a man, then I'm sorry to disappoint you. I'm not writing about *Clive Christian cologne, Christian Louboutin, Louis Vuitton, Jimmy Choo,* or any other shoe for that matter. This particular chapter is NOT about the latest gossip, *Remy* hair extensions, or *MAC* makeup. The truth of the matter, is that some of us have masked our issues with makeup.

We have perfumed our pain, deodorized our issues, and allowed the past to reign presently in our lives, offsetting the blessings of our future. So many of us have become desensitized, to believe that the more things we buy, the more friends we have, and the more money that we accumulate will alleviate the void in our lives and bring happiness.

JOY VS. HAPPINESS

If you're waiting for people and things to make you happy, you will be waiting for a long time. Some people can make you happy, but only God can bring you joy. You must realize that your value is not in what you have, your true value is immersed in who you are.

BEAUTY IS ONLY SKIN DEEP

True value and beauty, never originates from the outside-in, it always derives from the inside-out. A pretty face + a nasty attitude = an ugly person. The aforementioned is a problem, that must be solved.

Proverbs 31:10 affirms, "Who can find a virtuous woman? For her price is far above rubies." For the writer to even suggest, "Who can find?" means there's little supply and great demand. Your persona, gifts, character, intelligence, and goals should distinguish you from the masses because you are unique.

Recognize your gifts, value, inner beauty, and the treasure within you. Don't let anybody minimize your future, because of your past. You can't change the past, so why are you presently living in it? Stop beating yourself up over something that you can't change. Your experiences don't define you, they refine you and make you better.

THE (WO)MAN IN THE MIRROR

So many times we hide behind a mask, to mask the past. Take off the mask and begin to look within, the mirror of your soul. Many times we are afraid to address issues within, because it brings up old memories, scars, and hurt from the past. How can you heal from it, if you won't deal with it? Stop going through life numb and on auto-pilot.

Take control of your life, get in the drivers seat and press

forward on the road to your destiny.

Oftentimes whatever you are without, begins from

within. The outside won't fix the inside, until you deal

with what is on the inside first. When you work on

yourself from within, the true beauty of you will shine

through.

FORGIVE TO LIVE

Forgive anybody who hurt you and forgive yourself, for

allowing it to happen. You can't truly live, until you

forgive. I'm a living witness that forgiveness is freedom.

To forge ahead, you have to forgive and move past

anything, that's trying to keep you behind. Make a decision

that each day you won't be bitter, but you will strive to be

better.

ASSETS VS. LIABILITIES

It's critical that you surround yourself, with people who are assets to your life and not liabilities. If the people in your life are hurting you, putting you down, and bringing drama to your life then it's time to let them go. Your motto has to be, "If you can't add to my life, then I have to subtract you from my life."

In the matrix of relationships, we generally talk about the hurt that women experience from men, but we never talk about the hurt that men experience from women. You can cut somebody into pieces, with nonsensical words or build a man up as a nurturing woman.

Brothers when we truly show love to a woman and empower the queen in her, she will speak to the king in us. A true queen, speaks to the king in a man. Her beauty and effervescent pulchritude is not only on the outside, but it shines through from the inside-out. She is more than her assets, she is an asset. She doesn't compete, she complements her companion. In a world of quantity, she is a queen of quality.

Oftentimes, there is physical pain, verbal abuse, or even emotional hurt because of a relationship that left you broken. The incendiary effects of abuse and domestic violence, can destroy one's life and level of trust in relationships. When things become gender specific and chauvinistic, it leads to the ills within relationships to be ignored by both parties.

Only when you place your broken pieces in God's hands, then can you experience healing and peace to sustain your life. You will attract liabilities, as long as you continue to live according to the pain of your past. When you move from hurt to healing, you become your greatest asset and in turn attract people, who are assets to your life.

THE BLESSING OF RELEASING

Love yourself enough, to rid your life of toxic relationships. Some people you just have to bless and release. If we can't grow together, then I have to go without you. Your destiny awaits because power, promise, and possibility is on the other side of pain.

VIXEN OR VIRTUOUS?

Ladies, any real man will tell you that there's nothing more attractive than a beautiful, intelligent, sophisticated, goal-oriented, kind hearted, and spiritual woman whose life reflects love. A real man is not only concerned about the color and curves of a woman, he's impressed by the content of her character. The color that he's most interested in, comprises a heart of gold. The curve that is most endearing, is the one that forms when you smile.

Be the virtuous woman of value, that God created you to be. Never be the type of woman that needs a man, be the type of woman that a man needs. Your presence should affirm that you're not needy, you're needed.

Begin to become the type of person that you're looking for, because you will attract the type of person that you are. You will attract what you're thinking. If your mindset is negative, begin to change your thinking and you will change what you're attracting. You can easily find someone in the club or a vixen, but a virtuous woman is a rare jewel.

KNOW YOUR WORTH

Recognize your value and know your worth! Don't let the valuables on you, outweigh the value in you. Take off the mask and unveil the real you. Don't live your life, as a second rate version of who you are, when you were born to be a first class individual. You're pregnant with purpose, promise, and possibility. Now is the time, to give birth to the reality of your dreams and press past any obstacle that has held you back.

When you get a mental and spiritual makeover, it will radiate through your physical pulchritude and outward beauty. Transform your mind and your entire world will be transformed.

On your mark, get set, go...grow and glow from the inside-out. Inner beauty radiates more than makeup, self-love out shines any designer shoe, and inner healing is more priceless than a handbag. Begin to love, nurture, and see greatness in who you are. There is more joy, peace, love, and happiness that awaits you. Take off the superficial mask and begin to love the real you!

CHAPTER 5

Without Further "I Do"

So the song goes, "If you liked it, then you should've put a ring on it." The *Single Ladies* anthem seems to be more than just a pop culture catch phrase, echoing mellifluously and melodiously from Beyoncé Knowles-Carter.

Now if you've seen the video, you would be distracted by the calisthenics and gyrations, yet there is a message amidst the madness. If I asked the single ladies across America, to raise their hands, 51% of the women would acknowledge their unmarried status.

There was a popular saying in the 1990s, "You go, girl!" which was used as a term of endearment and encouragement. These days, the saying can be arguably rephrased to, "You go girl...and get married." A recent Yale study indicates that fewer women are walking down the aisle, as 23 percent of White women and 42 percent of African-American women have yet to be married.

SEEK AND YOU WILL FIND?

The wise saying in Proverbs 18:22 declares, "He that findeth a wife findeth a good thing, and obtaineth favor from the Lord." So, are men not looking or are they not finding? Looking and finding are 2 different things. You can be looking for something that you will never find, especially if it's a false pretense of the qualities in an individual.

According to Time Magazine's November 2010 issue, "Who Needs Marriage?" in the year of 1960, nearly 70% of American adults were married; now only about half are married. In 1960, two-thirds of 20-somethings were married; in recent years, just 26% were married.

TO MARRY OR NOT TO MARRY?

Is marriage becoming obsolete? Well, according to the Pew Research Center Survey, 4 in 10 say, "Yes." It is no secret, that approximately 60% of marriages end in divorce. The troubled state of our unions, indicate that marriage is becoming less popular in America. Why are 60% of marriages ending in divorce? For a myriad of reasons, as we have heard on talk shows like *Dr. Phil, Steve Harvey, Fix My Life* (Iyanla Vanzant), *The View, The Talk,* and a host of other programs.

FIX MY DATING/MARRIAGE LIFE

In chapter 3, "Love Under New Management" I suggested, did Tyler Perry get the question correct in his 2007 film asking, *Why Did I Get Married?* The question these days is not "Why did I get married?" but America is asking, "Why would I get married?"

MARRED MARRIAGES

As 60% of marriages end in divorce, 40% of people believe there is no need for marriage. Our country is at a crossroads. What has brought our nation to this point? Is the institution of marriage under attack and in the crosshairs within our country?

If we turn back the hands of time 50 years, it's amazing to see how popular culture mirrors society. We have transitioned from the wholesome households of The

Cleavers (*Leave It To Beaver*), *The Brady Bunch, The Cosby Show,* and *Family Matters* to now a false sense of Reality TV age. These days you see TV shows like *Basketball Wives, Love & Hip Hop,* and *Keeping Up With The Kardashians* style of living, dating, and marriage.

Going back some 50 years, many women had a degree in domestic engineering. Now it's the norm for women to specialize in fatherless home child rearing, in which mothers are told, "Happy Father's Day Mom" from children, who grow up in single parent homes.

The battle for the family is under attack. American culture shows the rapid transition in the familial landscape, as we have moved from *Family Ties* to *Divorce Court.* The Bible affirms in Mark 10:9, "What therefore God hath joined together, let not man put asunder." Yet we're putting our marriages asunder. So many have *jumped the broom* and used that same broom to sweep their issues under the rug.

COKE OR KARATS?

The woes of marriage is not excluded from our house, the White House, and even the church house. Can I get a witness? They met at church and began dating, you know how it goes. She dated thinking he was her Boaz, they got married and she discovered he was a bozo.

He thought she was the Biblical version of Ruth, but found out that she wasn't telling the truth. She had curves like the letter _"S"_ but the sister was really a snake. He was tall, dark, and looked like Morris Chestnut, but the brother was a nut. A friend of mine told me, "Just because she has a Coke bottle body on the outside, doesn't mean the pop ain't flat on the inside."

Quite hilarious, yet truthful. Indeed, we all have our perspectives and stories. Sadly, in a superficial society, we have become so focused on the size of the karats, that we have lost sight of substance and character.

How does your church deal with marital issues? Something is wrong, if we just continue to build churches and stand on the sidelines, while marriages are marred and families fall apart. It's one thing to build, buildings but it's another thing to build people.

TUNNEL VISION

Our society has gone from *Married with Children* to shacking up with children. The false sense of reality TV shows, with "Baby daddy and baby mama drama," continues to cripple our communities. I'm beginning to see the reason, why they call shows, "TV programs." The minds of our youth are so malleable that various programs, actually begin to program their minds. Oftentimes it's more negative, than positive. Many television programs have given Americans tunnel vision, while being mentally blinded by materialism.

I DO, I DON'T, OR I WON'T

For the record, *wifey* and wife are two separate functions. Yet in still, cohabitation is on the rise and since 1960, there are 8 times as many out of wedlock births.

How do you introduce the relevance of marriage, to an "I'm doing me generation?" Is it still possible to say, "I do" in an iPhone, iPad, iPod, and YouTube generation? We're living in a world today, that spells the word "We" with 2 _"I's."_ For all those living under a rock, I'm referring to the "Wii" video game system.

Even the names of our techno gadgets, are indicative of a narcissistic ideology. In an age that says, "It's all about I and you" can the focus still be on "We and us?" How can you build a long-lasting marriage, in an instant gratification society? People aren't waiting 7 years, to scratch their itch any longer.

If you desire to be married, what is your motive? Is it love, money, loneliness, sense of obligation, sex, control, age, etc?

A number of women flaunt their body, while many men parade their money. After the rendezvous is over she cries, "He only wanted me for my body" and he says, "She only wanted my money." Well, if that's only what you showcase and promote, then that is all you will attract.

If you don't remedy the damaging relationships of the past, it will bring about a jaded perspective for the future. Now when it's time for marriage, the man shouts like the Rapper Kanye West, "We want prenup, we want prenup." Read me clearly, "I'm not saying she's a gold digger, but she ain't messing with no"...I think you get my point.

Where is our value? What are your values? If you're exchanging your self-worth and character in hopes of karats, you will face the spectrum of disappointment. If you have to give an ultimatum, bribe her to be your bride, or beg a man to marry you, then you will have to do all of that to keep them from straying or leaving you.

I'm beginning to realize that marriage is not solely about finding someone that you can live with; it's about loving someone that you can't live without.

IT'S NOT A SPRINT, IT'S A MARATHON

In the societal 18-35 age demographic, is the spectrum of marriage only relegated to a woman being the envy of her girlfriends, or splashing her engagement ring on a social media page? What I'm saying is, do people only marry for the wedding?

Marriage is not a race, it's a pace. It's not a sprint, it's a marathon. It's best to be with the right person who is in shape spiritually, mentally, physically, interpersonally, and financially to go the distance with for the long haul.

There are some weeds that grow, after the wedding is over and if the garden of marriage is not pruned, then it won't last. Marriage is a merger and it's best to make sure that your life intersects and merges with the individual, before you trod down the aisle. You don't want to have an accident and crash into the wrong one, or you'll wind up saying, "What in the world did I get myself into?"

WHY DO FOOLS FALL IN LOVE?

Personally, I don't want to fall in love. I don't want to FALL into anything, that I can't get out of to save my life. I want to grow in love with the right woman. Even when things go left, if you have the right person on your team, your relationship and/or marriage will survive the storm.

In a marriage, the husband must be the house band and a wife should offset strife. I know they say, "Behind every good man is a good woman," yet a wife is better suited beside you, than behind you.

MARRIAGE IS A MERGER

We must think critically and evaluate ourselves, before we are betrothed to someone. Marriage is a merger and if you partner with the wrong person, the ramifications can be taxing. Marriage is not some type of taste test or product, with a money back guarantee.

Marriage is indeed a life-long investment, with it being akin to business. The symbolic consummation of marriage, is a merger and if you don't have the right partner, or make the right investments, your marriage will go bankrupt.

In the marriage liturgy, "Till death do us part" does not mean until things fall apart. We must be sincere, sure, and committed to be true, before we ever say the words, "I Do."

CHAPTER 6

Shut The Door

Back in the day, as a kid, I vividly remember walking into my mother's house, on freezing winter days and hearing her say, "Edward, shut the door all the way and don't let the heat out." Some of the simplest words you hear as a kid, takes on a new meaning as an adult.

The simple statement "Shut the door" can be applied to not only the temperature, but also the climate of our circumstances. Certain things in our lives have frozen us, out of the bright future that we seek to attain. Before you open the door to a new opportunity, you have to shut the door on toxic relationships, bad habits, and negative thoughts that keep you going in circles never making forward progression.

YOU HAVE THE KEYS

There is a door of opportunity that God wants you to step into, but it comes at the expense and even the pain of shutting the door on your past. Closing the door on your past, gives you the keys to open the door to your limitless future.

Shut the door on relationships that have kept you discombobulated, depressed, and defeated. It's simple to say, but it takes focus to do it. Shut the door and let go of negative thinking and low self-esteem. You have a gift inside of you that can turn stumbling blocks into stepping stones.

PAST IS PRISON, FUTURE IS FREEDOM

Your past is not a crutch, that you have to use to limp into your future. You can't walk or run into your future, if you're crippled by your past. When you free your mind, your future becomes a byproduct of your thought process. Remember that what's ahead of you, is far greater than what's behind you.

The frigidity of the world has infiltrated our mind and spirit, to the point that our dreams are frozen by fear and unbelief. Some of our hearts are frozen, due to past hurt from relationships.

Many of our lives are at a standstill, making no forward progression. Some people have left you out in the cold through broken promises, forsaking you in a time of need, or walking out of your life.

BETTER IS COMING

You can't afford to be bitter, because better is coming. Don't allow the pain of your past, to put an icebox where your heart used to be. God's love and self-love is strong enough to overcome apathy, bitterness, and hatred.

Rejection is direction, positioning you on the path of purpose. Every "NO" that you've been told, only means "New Opportunity." You have to look at the negative, positively and adjust your thinking towards victory and opportunity. Stop exposing yourself to the elements of negativity, apathy, and calamity. Shut the door of depression and step into a new place of peace. Shut the door of low self-esteem and step into a new place of self-love and serenity.

If people can't add to your value, then subtract them from your life. Don't forget, the past is a prison, but your future is freedom. Today make a decision to shut the door on everything that's holding you back, from becoming who you were created to be. Your future is an open door that awaits you. Shut the door, don't look back, move forward, and open the door to your destiny!

CHAPTER 7

Break Out

Who told you that you can't make it? What's holding you back and stopping you, from moving forward? You can't let what people say to and about you, push you off the path of your purpose.

People will YELL about what you do wrong and only WHISPER, about what you do right. At the end of the day, you are your only competition. Make a decision, to be the best YOU, that YOU can be!

BREAKDOWN OR BREAKTHROUGH?

How can you be the best, if you don't make adjustments? There is no growth without change. There are certain habits and people, that we need to break away from, so that we can breakthrough. Yes, old habits die hard but if you don't build good habits, then the bad one's will stifle your progress.

THE ONLY THING CONSTANT IS CHANGE

We must make the necessary changes to improve our health, relationships, and overall lifestyle. However, no changes will be made, if we don't change the way that we think. The way that you're thinking, has everything to do with where you're going, whether it be forward or backward.

There's an old-school song that says, "You've got me going in circles, round and round I go." This world is designed to keep you reaching but never attaining, just going in circles but never making any forward progress. Break free from drama, depression, negativity, bitterness, and strife. Break away from unhealthy and toxic relationships that are polluting your life.

You're too special and significant, to reduce yourself and succumb to the negative controls around you. It takes a resilient mind to make the quantum leap and break away from everything, that's trying to break you down. When you're dead, they're going to put you in a box, but since you're alive it's time to break out of the box!

ANALYZE AND ORGANIZE

The old adage suggests, "If it ain't broke, don't fix it." How can you improve your life, if you don't take inventory of your life? A lot of times we wait until things are in disarray to make changes, to the extent that we ignore the signals and red flags along the way.

Take time to analyze your life and your relationships. Who or what is a liability versus an asset? Don't wait until things are broken in your life, to remediate and repair certain issues. Do personal inventory and inspection. Break out of lethargy and take time to fix, mend, and repair before it breaks you.

BROKEN BUT BLESSED

You can be blessed, by being broken. Recorded in Mark chapter 6 is the story of Jesus feeding 5,000 people, with 5 loaves and 2 fish. Now mathematically this is impossible, because there's just not enough food for everybody.

However, when Jesus is in the mix, the laws of math don't matter. Before He disseminated the 5 loaves and 2 fish, He blessed it, and broke it. The more He broke it, the more people were able to be nourished by it. Now the laws of MATH would suggest, 5 loaves MULTIPLIED by 2 fish, would never equal feeding 5,000…yet Jesus continually DIVIDED the food among the people.

The more that you've been broken, the more pieces of your life you're able to share to strengthen somebody else. God will mend your life, to where you can find peace from broken pieces. Never discount yourself and doubt that you're blessed! Despite the breaking, God will use every situation to break you through. He will multiply your gifts, talents, resources, and life to bless others in the process.

God gave you a gift, now use it! Refuse to let people steal your joy, serenity, and strength. A knockdown is only a knockout, if you stay down. Get up, shake yourself, and get back in the fight. Break out of the box and bless the world, with everything that God gave you. You may be broken, but you can still breakthrough and break out, because you're blessed!

The world is waiting for you, to reveal the best of everything that's inside of you. Blast past your past, because what's ahead of you is far greater than what's behind you. Move forward and break out!

CHAPTER 8

Drunk In Love

Every Beyoncé fan recognizes the title of this chapter, knows the song, and needless to say, some sing it off-key! For those who don't know, this effervescent and intoxicating song, is composed of risqué lyrics and a pulsating beat. Beyoncé proudly expresses her affinity for her husband, Jay-Z.

There is a difference between like, love, and lust. Many times we become so caught up in a state of relational euphoria, ultimately clouding our minds, and confusing the qualities of love.

DANGEROUSLY IN LOVE

Be sober enough to recognize red flags…so you don't lose yourself in somebody, by failing to find who you are in the relationship. You can't be SOBER in love…if you're DRUNK in lust! Don't make a song your reality… maintain sober sanity, so you're not caught up in a state of drunk delusion.

When you're sober and sensible minded, you will raise your value and not hide it. When someone is lacking value and love within themselves, it's difficult to express it to somebody else. You can't express love, if you're filled with hate, depression, sadness, and dismay. How can you express, what you don't possess? How can you express what you haven't been exposed to?

OBEY YOUR THIRST?

Remember, don't TRIP over the red flags, just to FALL in love. You're too special, to just settle for anything. When you settle, you get less than you deserve. Don't become so parched and thirsty for love, until you let just anybody quench it. Don't lower your standards, just to say that you have somebody. Raise your value and your standards will follow.

Your life is a magnet and when you become a person of love…you will repel the WRONG ones and attract the RIGHT one! Ladies understand that a man's value, is not about what he can BUY you…but what he can INVEST in you!

Love doesn't mistreat and it's not filled with conceit. Real love builds up, it doesn't tear down. Love is strong enough to turn a breakdown, into a breakthrough. When you live and walk in love, it gives you laser-like focus to overcome fear and walk by faith. Love doesn't have a hand extended to TAKE from you, the hand of love reaches out to GIVE to you.

When God is managing your life, love will flow through your life, to bless somebody else. Don't let disappointments stop you, from believing in love and receiving love. The right person and the right relationship will make you realize, why the wrong one could have never worked in the first place. Love yourself before expecting it from somebody else. Invest in becoming the best, embrace your value, and know your worth. When you know your worth, you won't act like you're dying of thirst.

LOVE ON LIFE SUPPORT

In an ever-changing and evolving culture, it seems as if love is on life support. Materialism, militarism, and capitalism have become the norms of the day. The digital divide of technology, has divided us and the essence of true human interaction.

We hold our phones, more often than we hold hands. We know the apps, games, and photos on our phone and computer screens. On the contrary, do we know the color of the persons eyes or the laugh lines that form, when we bring a smile to the faces of those we love?

If love is on life support, then is chivalry dead? You know, courteous behavior…men opening doors for women, random acts of kindness, and ultimately courting/ dating with long term intentions. I know, who does that anymore, right? This sounds like a throwback episode of *A Different World* with the whirlwind relationship, of Whitley Gilbert and Dwayne Wayne (and for the record, I do wear those flip-up shades). As I stated previously, we are living in a different world.

Still in doubt? In the words of Rapper, Trinidad James, "Don't believe me just watch"…your TV screen, open your favorite magazine, and listen to the radio. As a matter of fact…scroll down your Twitter timeline, Facebook, or Instagram page. Now, do you see what I mean? It seems as if positivity, has taken a backseat to the negative.

Just the whole aspect of exemplifying ladylike and gentlemanly qualities, seems to be a novelty, a lost art, and quite uncommon these days in a culture moving at warp speed.

HOOK, LINK, HANG

Today's lingo is "Hook up, link up, and hang out." So, now relationships have become like the internet…Wi-Fi and high speed connections, with no strings attached. It's indicative of society, with fast food, fast money, fast cars, fast relationships, and life just moving too fast.

DÉJÀ VU

How we internalize the dynamic of relationships, begins with how we were raised. As I stated earlier, Sigmund Freud suggests, "We are in adulthood what we have experienced in childhood." Essentially, we are the products of early childhood development. Who we are, is directly connected to what we have experienced...the good, the bad, and the ugly.

However, our experiences don't doom or define us. We can define our experiences and use them to refine us, for the future. Shape your situation, don't allow your situation to shape you. Knowing the Master, helps you to become the master of your life and in turn...master life!

HEAL BEFORE YOU DEAL

In many cases, to DEAL with someone NEW…you have to HEAL the OLD wounds. You can't repel what you're attracting, if you're still the same person that's attracting the same people. Until you begin to love yourself, heal old wounds, appreciate your value, and endure growing pains, you will continue to attract the same OLD people in different places, with NEW faces. Realize that your life is a magnet. When you become a person of love, you will repel the wrong ones and attract the right one!

The same old wounds will open in a new relationship, if you don't heal from the old ones. You have to heal the old, before you deal with the new. When you heal it reveals greater vision within, to look at love through a different lens. When love begins from within, your parameters widen and you become a magnet for love. Heal you, before you deal with someone new.

In a subversive culture, we have become so focused and yes, even controlled by what we see physically. What's more important, getting to know her mind or her behind? His money or his personality? The book of Proverbs suggests, "A faithful man" and "A virtuous woman" are hard to find. Relationships, are much like the economic principles of supply and demand. If you invest in the wrong person, you can end up bankrupt. It's not too late to love yourself, appreciate your value, and know your worth!

Being a gentleman never goes out of style. Being a lady is more than fashionable, it's a lifestyle. You never have to become swayed by swag or style, if you lead and execute with class. Believe it or not, people are watching you and what you do. Raise the bar, set the standard, and inspire the next generation in the process.

UNDER THE INFLUENCE

Don't become drunk off delusions and trends. Live under the influence of love, healing, value, and respect for self. Live under that influence, helps you to be an overcomer and influence others positively.

As a result, you will begin to receive love and respect, from others in the process. Contrary to popular belief, chivalry is NOT dead...I'm holding the door open, for you to walk into your future!

CHAPTER 9

Grow Or Go

Y ou've heard the popular saying, "What doesn't kill you, makes you stronger." I like to say, "If it doesn't kill you, then use it to build you." Oftentimes, the greatest moments of strength, occur at our weakest moments of hopelessness and despair. It's true that we don't realize how strong we are, until being strong is our only option.

There is strength and wisdom within you, that you haven't used yet. There is a rich reservoir of resilience on the INSIDE, which is greater than what you possess on the OUTSIDE! When I battled stage 4 cancer as a teenager, I discovered that and gained strength through adversity. I had to find the strength to grow through life's obstacles!

WHO ARE YOU?

In life you will either be an eagle or a chicken, warrior or worrier, a champion or a chump! Which one are you? Many times, WHAT we become is predicated on WHO we surround ourselves with daily. Are the people that surround you, ADDING to you or SUBTRACTING from you? Are they helping you grow through or are they putting you through drama, mental angst, and unnecessary stress? Put your circle of friends and family under the microscope, to separate the contenders from the pretenders.

UNDER THE INFLUENCE

Everybody around you is NOT for you, some people are blocking you...let them go, so you can grow! Some people are wolves, in sheep's clothing. For those who are old-school, you know the O'Jay's called them *Back Stabbers*.

The lyrics suggest, "They smile in your face, all the time they want to take your place."

TAKE INVENTORY

Treat your relationships like a career profession, if they're a liability then fire them. If they're an asset then hire them, so you can go higher! At the end of the day it's nothing personal, it's just business.

For any business to flourish and thrive, it has to make good investments. The same principle is congruent to your relationships. Since you are the CEO of your life, you have to take inventory of your life. Realize your value, recognize your worth, and begin to invest in yourself. When you begin to do that, your relationships will yield fruitful results.

There are some people, who you just have to love from a distance. If they're an impediment to your life and not helping you grow, then you have to let them go! It's far better to be alone than in the company of bad people.

Negative people stunt your growth, positive people enhance your growth. Positive people will not disrespect you, they will help direct you to a place of greater growth. Surround yourself with people, who motivate you to be a better you!

I'M GROWING UP

You can't be your best, if you don't make improvements. The growth comes when you make adjustments. Just because you're grown, doesn't mean you're done growing. What I mean is that, growth goes beyond the spectrum of physical maturation. Growth is also interpersonal, spiritual, relational, and financial. Real growth helps to remedy the broken places, of our heart and mind, where inner-healing can begin. Take inventory, revisit the goals, focus on the plan, and believe that you can grow to the next level.

PLANT SEEDS OF SUCCESS

Like any seed, whatever soil you're planted in will either champion your growth or choke it. What you feed will grow and what you sow will show! For your relationships to flourish, there must be reciprocity. Make sure the people in your life, are sowing seeds of strength, by enriching, empowering, and encouraging you to grow to the next level!

GROWING PAINS

Everyone who you're connected to does not intend to give. The right people will do more than take from you, they will seek to add to you. Givers help you grow, takers stifle your growth. If they can't help you grow, they will have to watch you go!

There is no growth without change. It hurts to make change, that's why it's called *growing pains*. You will either experience the pain of discipline or the pain of consequence, as a result of your decisions. Some people GO through and stay in the situation. It's when you GROW through, that you come out! You know you're growing, when the situation that should have made you bitter ultimately made you better.

SHOW AND TELL

The right relationships will lift you up, not tear you down. Stop trying to see a new view of somebody, who showed you who they really are. Don't listen to what they say, at the expense of ignoring what they do. Remember they're telling you, simply by showing you. Don't get discouraged, God is saving you for someone special. He will send you the right message, to save you from the wrong people.

MORE IS IN STORE

There's more life to live, there's more dreams to transform into reality, there's more love to embrace amidst hardship, and there's more healing to experience in spite of pain! Whatever you're experiencing, be the rose that grows through concrete and blossom into the greatness that God has for you!

Believe that more is in store and the best is yet to come! Grow through every hurt, pain, and disappointment. Use it as fuel, to go to the next level!

CHAPTER 10

Love Don't Cost A Thing... Or Does It?

T he Atlanta, GA, Rapper T.I. in his song, *About The Money* emphatically declared, "If it ain't about the money, stop waisting my time." Is that what it's all about T.I.? This seems to be the consensus, of most people these days. Gone are the days, of people dealing in feelings or facts. The trend is to now only deal in figures.

WHO'S THE BREADWINNER?

Recently, I was in a male/female group discussion and a lady proposed a question, to the men. She asked us, "Would you be comfortable dating and/or marrying a woman, who makes more money than you?" The question posed to the guys, elicited a sobering reaction, with no initial response. Being in that room, you could hear a rat licking ice. Quiet. Nothing. Silence.

Of course, in jest and to lighten the mood, I flipped it back on her and said, "The real question is would she be comfortable, making less or even more than me?" During the discussion, a few of the guys expressed they would feel uncomfortable, if a woman made more money. The reason being, they would not be seen, as the *sole breadwinner* of the family. Some suggested that their egos would be bruised, as a result.

MONEY MATTER$

Ladies and gentlemen does it matter to you, who makes more money in a relationship/marriage? Kanye West suggested, "Having money is not everything, not having it is."

However, the majority agreed that relationships and marriage is about more, than what someone can provide monetarily. The person you are with, should support you spiritually, socially, and emotionally and inspire you to become better in the process.

If it's only about the money, bags, shoes, cars and clothes, then it becomes a superficial relationship. It's like building a house on sand, it can't stand. The true value in a relationship, is NOT about how many things somebody can BUY you…it's about how much they will INVEST in you!

BEAUTIFUL BAGS, BROKEN BAGGAGE

Your *Louboutin* shoes and *Birkin* bags, will get scratched and go out of style, but it's only real love that will remain.

Now, don't get me wrong, I'm not saying that it's wrong to have things. What I am saying, is that it's wrong when things have you. When the desire to accumulate things, becomes the focal point, then that's a problem.

Some relationships are filled with expensive gifts, but empty hearts. Beautiful bags on the outside, broken baggage on the inside.

You can't put a price on commitment, compassion, respect, loyalty, and honesty. You can't put a price on a good relationship, or a good marriage. You can't put a price on a good man, a good woman, and the value they bring to a relationship.

A WOMAN'S WORTH

Proverbs 31:10 affirms, "Who can find a virtuous woman? For her price is far above rubies." A virtuous woman's value is priceless, because she recognizes her worth from within. Essentially, if you can buy her, she's not the one. A woman of worth recognizes that her value is contained, by what's on the INSIDE rather than what she possesses on the OUTSIDE. You are not on SALE, don't let anyone DISCOUNT you! Your value doesn't come with a price tag, because you're priceless!

A woman of worth has value, because she's worth more than money. So contrary to the aforementioned song, for her it's more than about the money. Yes, being rich is a benefit, but it's not a necessity. Being with her is an upgrade and favor is a byproduct of it, because of her wealth within.

FROM LABOR TO FAVOR

A woman doesn't need a man to have favor, but brothers we need a wife to find favor. Proverbs 18:22 explicitly tells us, "He who finds a wife, finds a good thing and obtains

FAVOR from the Lord." When a man finds a wife his toil and labor, will immediately transition to favor!

LET THE EGO, GO

Much to my dismay, in our male/female discussion, a lady said, "Men are insecure about things regarding money and their egos can't handle, a woman making more than them." I immediately remarked, "All men are not driven by money and ego. Some are driven by passion and purpose."

As I thought about her statement, I realized that she expressed herself, based on her personal experiences or what she learned from somebody else. The most ego driven people are insecure from within, so they hide behind possessions and having things to validate who they are. The litmus test in a relationship should be, what CAN you offer that money CAN'T buy?

WHAT DO YOU BRING TO THE TABLE?

So many times, when relationships have gone awry, a woman cries and says, "He only wanted me for my body" and in anger a man says, "She only wanted me for my money." How can you expect them not to have an APPETITE, if that's all you bring to the TABLE?

Bring something to the table that the EYES can't see, so your HEART can discern, in order for your EARS to be receptive. Be more concerned about her CHARACTER than, her CURVES…be more focused on his WISDOM, than what's in his WALLET.

You're more than what you have, on the OUTSIDE. Look within, there's a great treasure of strength and beauty on the INSIDE of you. Let them see the true you, through your value. You are a blessing to somebody and if they don't recognize it, that's their loss!

THE RIGHT ONE

The right person will illuminate your ideas, empower you to think bigger, and speak to the greatness within you. When you meet the right one, your life won't be STRESSED…it will be BLESSED!

Don't get it twisted, you're not in a relationship or marriage for somebody to COMPLETE you…they should COMPLEMENT who you are. Never look for somebody to complete you, only God can do that. You don't need an opponent, you need a teammate. The right one will work with you, not against you. The right one won't COMPETE against you, they will assist you to complete the vision God gave you. Realize that God is preparing you for somebody and He's preparing somebody for you. Be patient through the process!

WHAT'S THE PRICE?

Real love doesn't step into your life to TAKE, it's on assignment to GIVE. Real love is not impressed with HOW much you have, it's focused on WHO you are. Recognize your value, love yourself through every circumstance, situation, and process so that you can look at your progress. Surround yourself with people, who invest in your value and love you through what you go through. Now that's priceless!

CHAPTER 11

Know Your Value

Would you like to receive a $100 bill today? First I must forewarn you, that it will be thrown on the ground, stepped on, tattered, torn, crumpled/balled up then placed into your hands. Now, do you still want this $100 bill? If so, why? Has the value of the money depreciated, because of what happened to it?

Of course, you would prefer a crisp/fresh $100 bill, but despite it's condition the value of the money remains the same. If money doesn't lose its value, which comes with a price, then it's worth knowing your value, because you're priceless! You are not on sale, don't let anybody discount you! You may have been stepped on, talked about, betrayed, bruised, abused, left for dead, or forsaken…but you still have value.

This is chapter 11 and it calls to mind, an individual or business filing for bankruptcy. More than economically, bankruptcy can affect us interpersonally. If you have no concept of your value, then you will always be bankrupt despite how much money you possess.

Realize and recognize, that what has been done to you, can't erase the value that is in you. Stop living your life to please people. Start pleasing God and everything else will fall in order. Never reduce yourself, to fit in with people who don't like you anyway. Make up your mind, to be everything that God created you to be in every way, everyday.

VALUE YOU

You're not worthless, you're priceless. Recognize your value! Your value isn't tied to WHAT people think about you, it's HOW you think about yourself! Don't let the opinions of others, interrupt the true thoughts of who you are...value you!

When you're driven by ego, you look for things to validate you. When you're driven by love, your value validates you. When you realize the God-given gifts within you, then you will realize your value.

NEW DAY, NEW YOU

As you know, every new year many people make resolutions (and maybe you do the same). Don't wait for a new year to make resolutions, when you can seize the moment each day and make transitions. Step out of the old and into the new.

YOU ARE WHAT YOU THINK

In order to do that, it begins with your mindset. Proverbs 23:7 affirms, "As a man thinketh in his heart, so is he." French philosopher, René Descartes remixed it this way and said, "I think therefore I am." Descartes expresses the fact, that you literally are the substratum of your thoughts and cognitive energy. Simply, you are what you think about. If you're thinking junk, you'll never become a jewel. How can you become wise, if you're thinking like a fool?

MENTALLY WEALTHY

You can't have a million dollar dream, with a bankrupt mindset. You can't have a rich life with a poor mindset.

Begin to think rich and become mentally wealthy. Realize that your thought life, will begin to attract what you desire.

You are not worthless, you're priceless. Don't let somebody who's blind to it, stop you from seeing your value. Don't become blind to the value in you. See value in yourself, appreciate who you are, and the right people will do the same. It begins from within! Be comforted in knowing, while God is preparing you for the right one… He's preparing the right one for you.

THE GREATEST INVESTMENT

Make an investment in yourself, there's value within you. When you invest in yourself, you'll see that your value is greater than anything you could ever purchase. Your value is not in what you have, it's in who you are. The value that you have on the inside, is greater than what is on the outside.

You're worth more than money, cars, clothes, and commodities. You're priceless! You will never go BANKRUPT, when you INVEST in yourself!

People will either add to your value, or subtract from it. If they're not adding, subtract them from your life. When you know your value, you surround yourself with people who enhance it...not diminish it. If they treat other people like trash, what makes you think they will treat you like a jewel? Don't place your value, in the hands of those who fail to realize it.

RECOGNIZE YOUR VALUE

Your value doesn't diminish, because somebody failed to recognize it. Don't lose your value, because somebody lost sight of who you are. You can't truly love, respect, and value somebody else until you love, respect, and value yourself. It's not about what you have, it's about who you are. Nothing you own on the outside, comes close to the value that you have on the inside.

If you don't recognize your value, why would anybody else? You may have been crushed and stepped on, but you still have value. It's worth knowing your worth!

CHAPTER 12

I've Got Issues

If you don't have any issues, then stop reading this book right now. If you're still here with me, then we're in this thing together. Simply because confession is good for the soul.

I'm not perfect and neither are you, but that's not an excuse for giving up and not striving to grow daily. The greatest growth and change, comes from recognizing our flaws and being inspired to get better each day. How can you change, what you won't confront? How can you heal from it, if you won't deal with it?

STAY HUMBLE

Just when you think you have it altogether, life will knock you off your high horse, to let you know that you're still human and you have plenty of room to grow. Proverbs 16:18, "Pride goeth before destruction, and an haughty spirit before a fall." Indeed the climb to success is challenging, but the fall from grace can be tragic.

1 Corinthians 10:12, "Let him who thinks he stands take heed, lest he fall." We must pay attention, take note, and take inventory of our lives. Look at the issues that we deal with and seek to heal from them. We all have issues, not dealing with them becomes a greater issue that complicates our lives and those who are in it.

The bruises and scars that you have are battle wounds, which express that you've been in a fight but you persevered to emerge victorious. Yes, you and I have been knocked down, but we're here because we didn't stay down. We got back up and fought to overcome.

S.O.S.

I know you have an <u>"S"</u> on your chest, because you see yourself as a *Superman* or a *Superwoman*. Yet beyond the surface that we see with our eyes, there's an S.O.S. tattooed on our hearts. The S.O.S. of *Save Our Souls,* speaks to a quest for the remedy, from the pain of the past.

The past pain often blurs the vision of our future. Yes, you may have been hurt, abused, neglected, and disrespected, but you don't have to settle for less. You don't have to engage in self-destructive behaviors, that offset the destined path of purpose, for your life.

We all have issues, but I'm a living witness that God has the healing tissues for our hurting issues. Jeremiah 8:22, "Is there no balm in Gilead? Is there no physician there? Why then is there no healing for the wound of my people?" God has the balm for our brokenness and the antiseptic of His anointing, can heal every hurting heart. His tender loving care can lift every burden, if we cast our cares on Him.

YOUR MESS IS A MESSAGE

Recorded in the Synoptic Gospels of Matthew, Mark, and Luke is the story of "The woman with the issue of blood." It's interesting that her affliction was public, but her name was private. Imagine going through life, being known for what's been done to you and the negative experiences that you've had.

Your mess overrides the essence, of the true message of your life. Would you want to be known as "The woman with the issue of abuse, neglect, or bad relationships?" How about being known as "The man with the issue of unemployment, addiction, or incarceration?" Like me, I'm sure you wouldn't want to be known for your issues, which would precede the powerful person that you are within.

A particular passage in Matthew 9:20, 21 declares, "And, behold, a woman, which was diseased with an issue of blood twelve years, came behind Him (Jesus), and touched the hem of His garment. For she said within herself, If I may but touch His garment, I shall be whole."

The woman had an issue of blood, for twelve years. We may not have the same particular issue that she had, but some of us have been carrying our issues for a long time. Oftentimes we go through life broken, hurt, angry, depressed, confused, and lacking love within ourselves. Imagine being in this woman's shoes. Even under the Mosaic law, which deemed her to be unclean. She was not allowed to come in contact with anybody, or they would be classified as unclean also. Yet in still, she pressed her way through the crowd to Jesus.

DO YOU HAVE THE RIGHT TOUCH?

She didn't touch Jesus, but she touched something that was touching Him. There was enough power in His garment, to transition her from sickness to healing. She had enough faith to push through her pain, to experience the power of healing. It doesn't matter how long, you've been carrying around your particular issue(s). If you take it to God, He will empower you to handle it and experience healing.

There are countless accounts of healing in the Bible. It's interesting that when men were healed, Jesus would restore their sight/vision. Every man must have a vision for their life, because it impacts their relationships and the decisions they make. Having sight but void of vision, just means you're still blind.

I CAN SEE CLEARLY NOW

Brothers, if we walk through life with the scales over our eyes blinded by our issues, we will never be the conduits of power in our communities. When you are a man with vision, God gifts you to produce, protect, and provide for the people that are in your life. Take off the scales and take off the mask, so that you can walk boldly into your future with vision.

As men received their sight to walk in vision, many women throughout scripture were afflicted with issues of infirmity. You may be asking, "How can I deal with my issues of abandonment, issues of abuse, issues of neglect, unsuccessful relationships, depression, disappointment, the hidden secret pains and hurts?" Nobody seems to hear your silent screams. Well, the Bible is full of women with issues, who found remedies:

THE WOMAN AT THE WELL

John chapter 4 highlights the woman at the well, who had 5 husbands. Also, the man she was living with, was not her husband. Jesus wasn't talking to her to spit game, but He came to restore her and give her living water. She was drawing from a physical well, but He wanted her spiritual well to never run dry again.

A MIGHTY GOOD MAN

She left her water pot, went into the city and said, "Come, see a man, which told me all things that I ever did: is not this the Christ?" The Hip-Hop trio, Salt-N-Pepa would say, "What a man, what a man, what a might good man."

Ladies, if a man can speak into your life, by empowering you to grow, and his actions align with his words…then he's a mighty good man. Don't make the mistake of only evaluating him, by how much money is in his pocket. Seek to draw from the wealth and value, in his mind and heart.

Don't get caught up in what car he drives, found out what's driving him. He could have an expensive car, wine you, and dine you…all at the expense of driving you into a life of hell, drama, and abuse. Discover his ambitions, what motivates him, and what is his vision. Focus more on becoming the right woman for the right man, instead of settling for a man right now.

Yes, my brothers as well, make sure that you look beyond her voluptuous body and find out if her lifestyle, aligns with your core values. Have enough vision, to see beyond what you see. You need more than a flesh mate, or a soul mate, you need a spirit mate. What your spirit needs, is greater than what your flesh desires. The right one will awaken the vision, dream, and spirit in you not just temporarily but permanently.

THE CRIPPLED WOMAN

In Luke chapter 13, the woman in the story could not straighten her body, look upward, or forward. The shape of her body, bent toward the ground for 18 years. Imagine having to walk bent over, for 18 years, much less 18 minutes.

Now, I've had back pains on a number of occasions and if your body is bent over, then you know it feels horrendous. Thankfully, my chiropractor gave me relief. However, it's another thing to deal with an infirmity for 18 years.

As it was, she could only see the dirt at her feet. She could only look downward and see the bad side of things. She could not look up and see the possibilities before her. She could not see the smiles on people's faces. She could not see the sky. She could only see downward to the dirt.

Sometimes life brings you so low, that all you trust is the dust. The cards of life can deal you a bad hand, to where you become pessimistic instead of optimistic. Despite what you have experienced, shake it off. Just because it's been that way, doesn't mean it will stay that way. You can change your circumstance, by thinking positive in a negative situation.

HEAVY ISSUES, HEAVY HEART

Can you imagine this woman? She could only look down, because she was bent over. Sometimes our issues weigh us down so much, that our physical body is impacted. How we feel on the inside, will impact our body and our expression on the outside.

Whatever is going on in our mind, will manifest throughout our body. You can only smile through pain, for so long before you breakdown. They say, "Fake it, until you make it." However, you truly won't make it, if you have to fake it. Rather, "Faith it, until you make it." Believe and walk in faith. When you become real with your issues, you will seek relief. It takes getting tired, of being sick and tired to find healing.

When Jesus saw her condition, he told her that she was free. She was free from the infirmity, that twisted her body into a deformed shape. Jesus declared, "Woman, thou art loosed from thine infirmity." Jesus put his hands on her and immediately, she straightened her body and was made whole.

HANDS OF HEALING

Ladies, a Godly and respectful man, won't use his hands to hurt or harm you. He will stretch his hands, to heal and help you! The woman with the issue of infirmity, received her healing. She could look upward and forward. It was not just her body that was healed, but her heart, and she praised God because of it. Her brokenness became her breakthrough. God can heal you and change your outlook on life. When He looses you, nothing can keep you bound!

For 18 years, the woman could only look downward. Since she was healed, her eyes could look upward and she could move around to see forward. Wherever you're looking, is an indication of where you're going.

Let your eyes and mind, be the engine that propels you, on the path toward your purpose. Keep your eyes to the skies. Psalm 121:1, "I will lift up my eyes unto the hills, from which comes my help. My help comes from the Lord, who made heaven and earth."

THE CANAANITE WOMAN

Recorded in Matthew chapter 15:21-28, is the story of a Canaanite woman, who had a daughter that was demonically possessed. She came and fell down at Jesus' feet. According to customs, they were not supposed to communicate. Simply because, Jesus was a Jew and the woman from Canaan was, who scholars suggested, a black woman.

AIN'T TOO PROUD TO BEG

The woman begged Jesus, to cast the demon out of her daughter. He replied to her, "Let the children first be filled: for it is not meet for me to take the children's bread, and to cast it unto the dogs." Maybe you missed that, but Jesus referred to the woman as a dog. Many would regard that connotation as offensive. I know a few people, who would've given Jesus a piece of their mind. Hold up, I'm from the east side, "Jesus you called me a what?"

However, as bold as Jesus' statement was, the woman's reply was even bolder. She said, "Yes, Lord: yet the dogs under the table eat of the children's crumbs." The woman could have expressed that she was offended, rather she looked past the offense and received her breakthrough. So much so, that her statement made the Lord holler, "O woman great is your faith, be it unto you as thou wilt" and her daughter was immediately healed.

DADDY'S LITTLE GIRL

I told you about the woman, with the issue of blood. Her healing is situated, within the story of the daughter of

Jairus, whom Jesus raised from the dead (Matthew 9:18-24). The 12-year-old daughter of Jairus, was physically dead.

The woman with the issue of blood had suffered for 12 years, from her illness and was deemed ritually unclean. Indeed Jairus' daughter was dead, but I would suggest that the woman with the issue of blood, was just as dead while being alive. To be existing and not living, is to be one who is dying.

WAKE UP

Jairus' daughter had lost her life. The woman with the issue of blood, had been unable to live a normal life, being ostracized and outcast from society. Therefore, she was dead to herself and the people within her circle.

Jesus restored, Jairus' daughter and the woman with the issue of blood, back to life. Before Jesus raised Jairus' daughter from the dead, he remarked "She is not dead, but is sleeping."

Only God can classify death, as an episode of sleep. I've got news for you, that your dream is not too dead, for God to resurrect it. His hand of love is on your heart and He is awakening, the giant within you to rise and conquer. You've been sleeping too long, on your goals and dreams. God is awakening you to rise, walk in purpose, and destiny.

ISSUES, ISSUES...IT'S YOU

It's quite interesting, that none of these women with issues had their names mentioned. Their issues outwardly, seemed to outweigh who they were inwardly.

I can hear people now, "Look that's the woman who got a divorce, that's the woman who lost her house, that's the woman who is sick and afflicted, that's the woman whose kid is strung out on drugs. There she is, there she goes, that's her right there." Sometimes we're recognized more by our issues, than by the value that is in us. Don't fret and focus on the issue. Focus on placing your issues in God's hand, He has a master plan.

The issues of dating, relationships, marriage, love, healing your heart, and overcoming your past are small in God's hands. Maybe you're saying to yourself, "How long will I be single, when will I get married? Time is ticking, and I want companionship." In your time of being alone, God seeks to make you one with him. You can be alone and not be lonely.

In a place of singleness and solitude, is an opportunity to continue to grow and work on yourself. Many times we see it as delay or denial, it's neither. God is orchestrating the right person and right opportunity, to collide with your destiny at the right time.

HIS BEST FOR THE BEST

How can God send you the right one, if you're still connected to the wrong person? He will not release His best, if you're entangled in drama and mess. Don't settle for a momentary substitute, when God has the right attribute to fit you, for a lifetime.

Do you have the discipline to wait and go through the season(s), where God is the potter, you are the clay, and He molds you each day? When you're the clay, you feel the potter working on the intricate places of your life.

No, it's not comfortable but it's necessary. It doesn't feel good now, but it's going to work out for your good in the end. Trust Him through the process. Stop looking for somebody to complete you, only God does that. He's not giving a half person, to a whole person. He wants you to be healed, but you have to place the brokenness and shattered pieces of your heart, in His hands.

So often we fail to see our own brokenness, because we're pointing the finger and looking for flaws in everybody else. Before analyzing and criticizing somebody else's issues, look at your own first. Grandma would always say, "Sweep around your own front door, before you try to sweep around mine." She is a Southern sage, with contemporary truth.

You've been carrying around more baggage, than the cargo on an airplane. Being in a relationship is like boarding a plane, too much baggage is going to cost you. When you go through life broken and weighed down, your dreams won't take flight. God wants you to cast your cares on Him, because He cares for you. Throw all of your issues at Him and He will empower you through them. What you're going through is only an indication, of where you're going to. The greater the battle, the greater the blessing.

Throughout scripture you can find Jesus, asking those who were sick with infirmities, "Wilt thou be made whole?" In other words, do you want to get well? Are you sick and tired, of being sick and tired? When they were healed, He would say, "Your faith has made you whole." To heal your heart, it takes faith and an unwavering will, to overcome every issue that seeks to debilitate your life. It's your faith, your belief, and your mindset that will birth healing from within.

TOO LOOSED, TO BE BOUND

Jesus told the crippled woman in the book of Luke, "Woman thou art loosed." Confess over your life that you're loosed from abuse, loosed from your past, loosed from the pain of brokenness, loosed from low self-esteem, loosed from depression, bitterness, and anger. You are loosed to walk in liberty and love!

As you're reading this chapter, maybe you're saying, "Why the Ladies and the accounts of women being healed?" I'm so glad that you asked. I believe there is something intrinsically special, about how a woman is designed.

I heard someone say, "When God created Adam, He was just a rough draft but Eve was the final copy." What we lack as men, women make up for and yes, vice versa. One of the greatest entertainers of all time, James Brown, sang "This is a man's world, but it would be nothing without a woman or a girl."

The sensitivity, compassionate, nurturing love, and care of a real woman is expressed in her actions. Before Eve was ever presented to Adam, he was given responsibility to tend the garden, which was his j-o-b.

Adam had a personal relationship with God. He had everything in order, before Eve came on the scene.

WAITING TO EXHALE

When God created Eve, she was never taken from the head of Adam to be superior to him. Eve wasn't taken from Adam's foot to be beneath him. She wasn't taken from His back to be behind him, but she was taken from the rib of Adam's side to surround and stand beside him.

If you study the anatomical structure of the human body, you will discover that your ribs protect your lungs, which assist in breathing. Brothers, when we find our rib, we'll be able to inhale and exhale a lot easier. However, if it's the wrong one, she will give you asthma and emphysema.

God will release to us what we're in need of, when we release from us what is not needed. A lot of times in church, the Pastor will preach from the book of Ruth, including the love journey with Boaz. As a result, many single women begin to get encouraged, to stand in faith for their Boaz to marry them.

Faith for a husband is all well and good, but ladies God isn't giving you a Boaz, until you let go of that bozo. God is not sending you his best, to compete with the rest. If you're willing and able, God is ready and willing.

RELATIONSHIP ECONOMICS

Sometimes what is best for us, is right in front of our face. Yet, because they don't fit our fantasy or description, we ignore them. He may not be a millionaire, but if he has the mindset of a millionaire, it might be worth the investment.

Relationships are not take, take, take, and take some more. They are rooted in giving for reciprocity. If you connect to his vision, and 2 become 1, then you can multiply your resources by investing in one another. I'm not saying lower your standards or ideas for a relationship and marriage, just explore them a little further. Delve a little deeper. When you understand the laws of relationship economics, you will realize the principles of investing in someone's value, that reaps benefits.

FAITHFUL, FLAWED, FOCUSED

Sometimes we have to weigh, vanity versus value and substance, in juxtaposition with style. Think about your flaws, in dichotomy with the flaws of others.

There are no perfect people. We are imperfect people, striving for perfection. As you know, it's a process. Despite your flaws, stay focused, faithful, and committed to becoming a better you. Take time to think and work through every issue. God will flip the script and use them to bless you.

CHAPTER 13

DIVAS

O
n many occasions, I speak to groups of women
on college campuses, at conferences, seminars, and
workshops. I generally open by saying, "To all the DIVAS
gathered here today, these Divinely Inspired Victorious
Accomplished Sisters."

Indeed that's how I define who DIVAS are and what
they do. I believe in uplifting the women in our culture,
communities, and churches.When you think of that title,
many talented artists like Aretha Franklin, Diana Ross,
Mariah Carey, and Whitney Houston come to mind. The
definition and perspective of DIVAS, goes beyond women
who are world-renowned singers and entertainers.

SHE'S EVERY WOMAN

DIVAS are entrepreneurs, nurses, doctors, lawyers, teachers, beauticians, domestic engineers, and all around leaders. You can't deny the power that women have, especially in a society that is ever-changing. Women are leaders in technology, business, entertainment, education, and sports.

Even throwing like a girl, isn't so bad these days. The mega-talented Mo'ne Davis, became the first girl in Little League World Series history, to pitch a winning game for the Taney Dragons. Who knows we may even have a First Lady of the United States, become the first female President of the United States of America. The hand that rocks the cradle, may rule the free world.

GIRL POWER

As we see the rise, power, and advancement of women in society, many still don't recognize their power in a relationship. Not the power to control a man, or make others concede to your every wish.

I'm referring to the innate power, to attract what you want and the type of person that you desire, through the character and qualities that you exude. It's of none effect, to be powerful publicly and powerless privately. Real DIVAS know the value that they possess and as a result, create empowering standards to live by daily.

I often tell women, "Always keep your standards, higher than your heels." People will treat you, according to the standards that you set and put into practice for yourself. The standards that you set, will elicit the respect that you receive, or lack thereof. It's more than lip service, it has to be expressed in your lifestyle.

As you have read many themes throughout this book, hopefully you have begun to adopt a new mindset in the process. This is your greatest opportunity to live, love, and heal from broken relationships, lifting your life to a new level.

3 TYPES OF PEOPLE

Within the matrix of relationships, a majority of people fall into 3 categories:

1. **Those who don't know what they want.**

2. **Those who don't get what they want.**

3. **Those who know what they want and when they get it, they don't want it.**

Do you fall into any of these categories?

1. Those who don't know what they want.

One thing you have to know, is what you want. Whether that's in a career, relationship, or simply ordering from the menu at dinner. If you're indecisive, someone will make a decision for you. The decision will generally be what you don't want, because you haven't expressed what you do want. Yet how do you know what you don't want, if you don't know what you do want? Quite puzzling indeed.

So you say, "Well, I just want someone to love me and treat me like a queen." Okay, so the man showed up to do both of those things, but you didn't want him. A lot of times we are indecisive, because we fear rejection. We don't want to hurt others, but we don't want to be hurt either. Also, because we have been hurt, now our guard is up and we're suspicious of everybody.

FEAR MAKES YOU INFERIOR

Don't let fear stop you, from going for what you truly desire. Fear will stifle your future, if you let it fester in your mind. A lot of times, we don't know what we want, because we haven't figured out who we are. We're waiting for a relationship to define us, a certain amount of money to bring us a sense of value, or accomplishments to lift our self-esteem. Eleanor Roosevelt said, "No one can make you feel inferior, without your permission."

Stop giving people the consent and power, to make you lower your expectations and belief within yourself. It begins with you, not them. What do you desire, what are your interests, goals, and aspirations? What type of person are you attracted to? What qualities to do you exude, to attract that type of person? Begin to decide what you want. Not living impulsively or with a "Whatever's clever" mindset, because you will get whatever if you don't identify what you want.

2. Those who don't get what they want.

You say, "Well I know what I want, but I'm not getting it." What are you doing, that is stopping you from attaining it? You will continue to get what you don't want, if you keep focusing on what you don't want. Change what your focusing on and you'll change, what you're receiving in return.

LOVE LANGUAGE

If you keep saying, "All men are dogs and they're just after one thing," then you've put that out into the universe. So guess what, only (as George Clinton would say) the atomic dogs and one-track minded men, will come barking and running after you. There is a law of attraction and there is also a law of language. Whatever you're speaking and thinking, will eventually come knocking at your door. Your cognitive thoughts and confession, will bring the manifestation of your actions.

Proverbs 18:21, "Death and life are in the power of the tongue." Begin to develop your love language. Begin to confess and profess, that you will have the best.

Another statement I hear is, "There are no good men out here." No, you're just not attracted to the ones who are good men, or you're not attracting them. Sometimes I hear women say, "Well, he's just too nice." Huh? Excuse me? I would hope that you don't want an irresponsible male, to disrespect you and treat you less than you deserve. Notice, I didn't call him a man.

There's a stark difference between a male and a man, just like there's a difference between a female and a woman. A real man or woman, walks in their God-given gift through respect and responsibility. They set standards for themselves, because they recognize the value of self and service to others. A grown male or female only operates in their gender, irresponsibly and has not come to the awareness of self, to live on a greater level. Gender doesn't make you a man or a woman. Only respect, self-love, and responsibility can usher you into that arena.

What differentiates you from the masses? What is unique and valuable, that you possess from within? I'm not talking about your curves and voluptuous physique. If you live long enough, all of that will fade and sag. What do you have of value, that can't be seen? What distinguishes you from everybody else.

QUALITY VS. QUANTITY

There are plenty of 7-Eleven convenience stores, but there are fewer 5-Star restaurants. If everyone else is a thrift store, you've got to be *Bloomingdale's*, *Neiman Marcus*, or *Saks Fifth Avenue*. Realize that quality, is greater than quantity. You always appreciate more, what you can't get at every store. Such is life, you appreciate and celebrate the quality people, that you can't find on every corner, club, and community.

There are 7 billion people on the planet, that's quantity. Connecting with the right person, that recognizes your value and loves you, that's quality. You can't ignore the fact, that your life is a magnet. Essentially, you will attract the type of person that you are.

Oftentimes isolation is an avenue for preparation. Are you preparing, while you're waiting? The *waiting* word does not mean, sit and do nothing. When you're waiting, it's like waiting as a waiter, instead of waiting on a bus. While you're waiting don't stand idly by, but keep working for what's coming. Great things are in store for you, if you stay true to your purpose.

INVEST IN YOU AND HE WILL TOO

Most men would agree that we like sports, a woman that is attractive, can cook, goal oriented, nice personality, keeps her appearance up, etc. DIVAS, take time to go to the gym and work on your physical pulchritude.

There is no doubt, as men we are visual. So be attractive, not attracting and leave something to the imagination. Spend some time pampering yourself, keeping your hair, and nails done. Perfect your cooking skills. Learn about the major sports: football, basketball, and baseball. Invest in yourself! Don't just work on the outside, but develop the immaterial part of you, which can't be seen with the naked eye.

A beautiful woman with a great personality and an intelligent mind, is the prototype for a man, who is not insecure. Develop your mind by reading books, attending seminars, enrolling in a class, learning a new skill, and working to improve yourself daily. A woman who invests in herself, will always have options and not be subject, to the decisions of others for her life.

DIVAS, when a man sees you investing in yourself, he will be intrigued about investing in you. Don't get it twisted, I'm not referring to what he can buy you. I'm speaking to the value, that he can add to you. No number can add or multiply, exponentially on its own, it needs something of equal or greater value to affect the sum of its substance. The right person will be an asset to you and add to your value. When you meet the right one, you're either going to be ready or trying to get ready. If you stay ready, you won't have to get ready.

3. Those who know what they want and when they get it, they don't want it.

Like they say, if you're looking for an excuse you will find one. If you're looking for the imperfections in others, you will find those too. While we're looking at everyone else's imperfections, we seemingly glance over our own and remain blind to what we do. You may say, "I want somebody who's in shape, has a million dollars, big house, and a foreign car." Well, do you have any of that? What shape are you in financially, mentally, physically, and spiritually? Essentially, what are you bringing to the table, other than an appetite?

RELATIONSHIP ENTREPRENEUR

If 2 business executives were sitting at the table, to discuss a merger, each person would have something to bring to it.

Why would a relationship be any different? Relationships are a lot like business, it can't be all one sided. Bring something to the table to give, not just to take. You will get more out of it, if you extend hands to give, instead of clenching them to take. Become a relationship entrepreneur, that does more than take but rather takes steps to sow, grow, and invest in someone else.

Learn how to build a friendship, before seeking a relationship. The foundation can't stand on sand, put some brick and mortar to develop the standards, structure, and building blocks towards what you envision. The most compatible and ideal companion, may sometimes be the friend that you overlook.

GREAT ISN'T GOOD ENOUGH

Have you ever known somebody, when no matter what you did for them, it was never good enough? No matter what you did, they were never satisfied. Let me tell you, it's not you that was the issue, it was them. For some, your great will never be good enough.

If you're not satisfied with yourself, nobody will be able to satisfy you. If you can't be alone and enjoy your own company, don't expect anybody else to enjoy your company either. You will treat people, according to the reflection that you have of yourself. What do you see, when you look in the mirror? See yourself as a leading lady of liberty. Look at your life in *3D*, as a *Divine Daughter of Destiny*!

TOY STORY

Don't let anybody treat you like a toy, that involves games, tricks, and schemes. Don't let them play with your emotions, wind up your expectations, twist you in a trap, and treat you like a joker. You're not some toy, that when after someone ripped off the wrapping paper and played with the object, now they're bored and don't want it anymore. You're not some object, that somebody can just pick up and put back on the shelf. God bought you with a price and you are priceless,

(I Corinthians 6:20).

You are not a toy but a treasure, that must be valued, because of the gift that God placed in you. You can't place yourself in everybody's hands, because people will mishandle you. People will drop you, bruise you, and break you without any consolation, remedy, or conscience of their mistreatment. You will look up and you find yourself, trying to recover from years of pain. You're a gift to somebody, and if they don't recognize it that's their loss!

Realize that you're never too old, to be inspired by a children's major motion picture. In the movie *Toy Story*, the character *Buzz Lightyear* reminds us, that we are on the path, "To infinity and beyond." Lay aside everything that weighs you down, so your dark night can manifest into a light year. It's a new dawn and a new day in your life. This is your time to walk in the light of love, healing, hope, and prosperity.

Don't let anybody, become a barrier to your breakthrough. Just like the movie suggested; you're *beyond* drama, *beyond* brokenness, *beyond* depression, *beyond* low self-esteem, *beyond* abuse, and *beyond* bitterness. Get to the *beyond* stage of your life, so that you can walk into the bright path of your future.

GET YOUR LIFE

So many times, we would rather hold on to the wrong person, just to say "I have somebody," instead of holding out for the right person because of a waiting period. If you're not healed from within and you meet the right person, you won't know how to handle them. You can't embrace what you want, if you haven't accepted what you need.

The singer, Lauryn Hill asked us the pertinent question, "How are you gonna win, when you ain't right within?" Much like chapter 1 of *Heal Your Heart* suggested, your development and progress in life begins from within.

WHO CAN FIND?

I'd like to say that DIVAS, are also Divinely Inspired Virtuous Anointed Sisters. They are not trying to compete, they are seeking to complete the work that God has intended for their lives.

Proverbs 31:10 asks, "Who can find a virtuous woman? For her price is far above rubies." In essence, if I can buy her, then she's not the one. Notice, the scripture never asked, "Who can find a vixen?" You won't find that, but you will find a virtuous woman as the quality of person required.

Proverbs 20:6 also affirms, "Who can find a faithful man?" For the writer to include that assertion, means there's little supply and great demand. Gospel singer, VaShawn Mitchell would say, "I searched all over, couldn't find nobody. I looked high and low, still couldn't find nobody."

Never go into a relationship, if you're not healed. You will always make bad choices, when you choose from weakness rather than strength. You never want to lower your standards, just for the sake of having somebody.

Waiting for what you want, is better than settling for what you don't want. I'm telling you like the singer Tamar Braxton, "Get your life!" Don't let your life slip away and fall into the hands, of somebody who doesn't know your worth. When you're going to the next level, you can't afford to settle. Aspire to attain the best and nothing less!

HOW TO KEEP WHAT YOU HAVE

I hear many ladies say, "I want a hard working man. However, after you get the man, how hard are you willing to work to keep him?"

Now that you've got the ring, you stop exercising. What happened to the home cooked meals? You don't make the macaroni and cheese, like you used to and the cornbread is now burned.

If cooking was your thing to get him, don't stop cooking now that you have him. Whatever you did to get him, you're going to have to do the same thing to keep him. Watch what you do, before you say, "I do."

Just because you're married, doesn't mean you have to stop dating…your husband or wife. Rekindle the fire and keep the excitement going. Remember it's not a sprint, it's a marathon.

THE GENESIS OF A GENTLEMAN

By nature, men are hunters. We are naturally competitive and seek a challenge. It's who we are, it's in our DNA. So it goes like this, "If you run I chase, but if you chase I run." Ladies you will continually be out of breath and your feet will always be tired, if you're chasing a man. Stop chasing a man, who doesn't want to be caught.

Like they say, "We adore those who ignore us and we ignore those who adore us." Oftentimes a man pays attention to the woman, who's not paying attention to him. He's looking, but you're steadily focusing, on working and handling your business. Some men would find that type of woman attractive.

Instead of being the person who's in somebody's face, take the time to invest in yourself and your career. Don't be a gold digger, be a goal digger. Let a man find you, reaching for your goals and dreams instead of his dollars.

The Genesis of a gentleman, emanates from his connection to God, an understanding of self, and the value that he brings to a relationship. Opening doors, kind acts of chivalry, communication, respecting, and treating a woman like a queen is rooted in his character. He seeks to protect a woman's heart and love her through adversity.

A man is not a construction project, stop trying to fix him. If he doesn't want to treat you right or pay attention to you, then you can't convince him otherwise. Only God can change someone. Some of us go into relationships and waste our time, trying to change people. If God hasn't changed them, then you surely can't change the person who God made.

BETTER TOGETHER

The singer Ne-Yo said, "I'm a movement by myself, but I'm a force when we're together." There is much truth within his lyrics and that is, the right woman is a help meet. In essence, she makes him better, because they're together.

Eve was Adam's help meet. The word *help meet* doesn't mean, help to meet the bills. The term denotes, someone who is compatible and on your level. Not just physically but spiritually, intellectually, and socially. The right person will do more than verbally compliment you, they will personally complement you.

A DIVA realizes that her personality and presence as a woman, supersedes her pulchritude and outward adornment. She understands her value on the inside, that permeates who she is on the outside. A woman's personality and presence, should be like potpourri to a room. More than beauty, her attitude should be a fragrance, not an odor.

Don't let a beautiful face, be ruined by an ugly attitude. Personally, I'm not so much concerned about a woman's color and curves, as I am the content of her character. When you can get both, that's a dynamic synergy.

In the movies, music, and relationship conversation, we always hear about love at first sight. I don't believe in love at first sight, I believe in like and lust at first sight. Beyond attraction, you truly can't love someone you don't know. Take time to go through the seasons with a person.

Yes, Spring, Summer, Winter, and Fall. People change with the seasons, so pay attention to the changes.

One of the biggest mistakes that you can make is to settle, just to say you have somebody. Sometimes the one you're with, is not the one God wants. Ask yourself, "If I join forces with this person, will I be in the red or the black? Are they an asset to me or a liability for me?"

As you invest in yourself, begin to pamper and keep yourself up. Enhance yourself holistically. There's nothing like a woman, who keeps a manicure/pedicure, goes to MAC to do her makeup (not heavy), and she can make some mean macaroni and cheese.

DATING AND DATA

Date with direction, purpose, and use that data to make a decision. In other words, seek to get information. Don't become inspector gadget, just learn to observe, communicate, and listen. Don't become so on edge or desperate, that you're seeking to get married on the first date. Before trying to jump the broom, use that same broom to sweep up the dust from your past.

One of the most powerful passages of scripture is Romans 12:2, "Be not conformed to this world: but be ye transformed by the renewing of your mind." However, I cannot present my body, until my mind has been renewed. Simply because, if I have not been transformed by God's Word, I will remain conformed to the world. Indeed and in fact, none of us are perfect, but all of us can be genuine.

God will never bring anyone into your life, that divides you from your destiny. They will either add or multiply to your purpose. If they are trying to divide you from your destiny, subtract them from your life. Genesis 1:28, "Be fruitful and multiply." Every man should be able to do one equation, and that is multiply your life. The wrong one, will subtract or divide from it.

Every man wants a woman whose presence says, "I'm not needy, I'm needed." We always focus on, what we can do for somebody or what they can do for us. The real question is, what can you do with them? Can you communicate with me, can you pray with me, and can you encourage me?

SAME ISSUES, DIFFERENT FACES

Some of us are in a new relationship, with the same old person. Sadly, the only thing that changed, was the face. Who you're attracting has more to do with you, then it has to do with them.

You will attract the same type of person, if you're the same type of person. The quality of person that you're attracting will change, when you change. In essence, you will attract who and what you are in life. The truth is a hard pill to swallow and many will not digest it easily.

You will attract people of value, when you invest in yourself, beyond what the eyes can see. Recognize your value and know your worth. Take inventory of your life and analyze it. Relationships are the glue for life. If you're a hater, bitter, negative, and nasty then those are the kinds of people, that you will attract.

An aphorism suggests, "We don't attract what we want, we attract what we are." If you're attracting the same old person, it's because you're the same old person. When you're a genuine person, you attract genuine people.

Do your relationships continue to fail, do people mistreat you, fool you, bruise you, and leave you broken? Then you have to get to the point, where you ask yourself, "Why are all these different people, doing the same thing to me?" Realize that it has nothing to do with them and it has everything, to do with you.

TRICK OR TREAT

The way people treat you, is based on the permission that you grant them, in your relationships. Yes, people may enable and mistreat you, but ultimately, it boils down to whether you deny or allow it to happen. They will never treat you right, if you keep allowing them to trick you.

Yes, everybody plays the fool, but the tragedy is remaining a fool. Don't let anybody cast you, for a starring role, to play the fool in your own lifetime movie. Every lesson is a blessing, so learn from your mistakes.

If you keep making the same mistake, then it's no longer a mistake but it's a decision. Be more wiser, than you were foolish. Never do permanent things with temporary people, because it can leave permanent scars.

The scars, bruises, and brokenness that our hearts have

incurred, need healing in order to experience real love.

My dear DIVA, my beautiful sister, lift up your head

and look into the mirror of your life. You are beautiful!

Your past may be marred in pain, but your future is bright

as the sun!

DIVA TO-DO LIST

When you're poised, purpose driven, and passionate, then

things will fall in place. Here are 6 essentials, that every

DIVA needs, to be a woman of grace and greatness:

1. A Book - Write A New Chapter.

Take time to read, invest in yourself, and deposit

knowledge into your mind. Educate, empower, and

encourage yourself on a daily basis. A woman who is

knowledgeable about her world, current events, and has keen wisdom, is indeed a jewel. Real DIVAS, cultivates their intelligence daily. Spend time researching, studying, and absorbing insightful information. Remember that your next chapter, is greater than your last one. Keep writing your story of strength and success. The book of your life, will help someone breakthrough.

2. Mentor And Model.

There should be someone in your life who mentors, motivates, models success, and helps you to manifest your destiny. You're never too old, to have a mentor. You need to be accountable to someone, who challenges and inspires you to succeed. As a result of your wisdom gained, take time to pay it forward, and help someone along the way. You may never be *America's Next Top Model*, but you can be America's next top role model.

3. High Standards In High Heels.

What DIVA doesn't own a pair of heels? No, they don't have to be *Giuseppe Zanotti* or *Manolo Blahnik* shoes. Any pair of heels will do, to symbolically walk out of your past and into your future. Psalm 18:33, "He makes your feet like hinds' feet and sets you upon high places." Step on the negative, use your haters as elevators, and go higher.

Stop focusing on the women who don't like you, or the man who didn't love you. You're not wearing gym shoes, to chase after a man. You are wearing heels, to walk in purpose and materialize the plan. You're a DIVA, so keep stepping into success. Strut with high standards and high goals, in high heels!

4. Bank Account/Purse - Pursue Purpose.

I'm not telling you to go out and purchase a *Birkin* bag, because you could place that money in your savings account. I never said to get a *Miu Miu* bag, because you knew that it didn't take all of that, to express your DIVA qualities.

In her song *Bag Lady*, Erykah Badu said, "Bag lady you gone hurt your back, dragging all them bags like that." Stop carrying around bags of hurt, abuse, bitterness, and brokenness. Begin to lighten your load and rid yourself, of things that weigh you down. It's a designer bag, but the stuff that you're carrying inside of it, is often designed to breakdown.

Stop waiting on a man, start working your vision and plan. Do more than chase money, chase your purpose. When you chase purpose, money will chase you. When God's favor is on you, financial blessings will follow you. Blessings are a byproduct of those who become a blessing, rather than worrying about how to get a blessing. Start becoming, what you're in anticipation of receiving. See your true beauty and inner wealth, as you heal yourself.

Invest from within and you will never go without!

5. A Pair Of Jeans.

Look through your closet and grab a pair of old jeans. Preferably a pair that makes you proud, of the weight that you lost. Now applaud your progress, celebrate your success. Yes, health is wealth and sometimes you gain by losing. Just like those old pair of jeans that don't fit, it's a reminder that old relationships don't fit you anymore and old habits can't invade your life. Now, if they still fit, then you've got some work to do.

Oftentimes you become a winner, by being the biggest loser. Lose those fake friends, lose that nasty attitude, lose low expectations, and lose a negative mindset. It's okay to lose certain things and never find them again. Sometimes a loss, is the greatest gain.

6. Self-Love.

DIVAS, the social media site is called FACEbook for a reason…stop showing your BEHIND! Your name isn't *KFC* or *Popeyes*, don't relegate yourself to breast, hips, legs, and thighs. How can you get upset, if the same type of male approaches you, when you're only showing them one thing? Remember, you will attract, that which you put out into the universe. Don't call him "Thirsty" if you're parading your body, like a beverage that will quench it. Don't expect him to not have an appetite, if all you're bringing to the table is meat.

What can you offer the world, that's more than a pretty face and a slim waist? It's time to let the true value within you, shine through. When you understand your worth, then you'll know that it's not about how voluptuous you are, it's about how virtuous you remain. It's not about how many "Likes" you get on Instagram, it's about how much love you have for yourself and the common man.

You can't expect anybody to love you, if you don't love yourself. The love that you're seeking on the outside, will never be realized until you heal and fill yourself, with love on the inside. Love doesn't come to take, love comes to give. You are special, valuable, and beautiful in God's sight. When you love God, He shows you how to love yourself.

CHAPTER 14

Change Is Gonna Come

People always talk about embracing change. Let's be honest with ourselves and affirm that change hurts. I don't know about you, but it hurts to eat differently, change old habits, and do what you don't feel like doing. How can you heal, if you won't keep it real? Yes, even the truth hurts, but it will set you free. People will hate the truth and fall in love with a lie.

They say "Old habits, die hard" because change is not easy. I'm convinced that people don't like change, because it hurts to break out of your comfort zone and cycle of old habits. Aren't you tired of a new year but the same old, same old?

You will remain in a cycle of self-destructive behavior, if you don't change your mindset and break out of the box. The reason people do what they do, is because of how they think. What you're doing and where you're going, has everything to do with what you're thinking.

YOU CAN'T NUMB THE PAIN

I wish there was an anesthetic for change, so I wouldn't have to feel the peaks and valleys of transformation. Don't you just wish you could wake up from the anesthesia and there be no more struggle, temptation, obstacles, or thoughts of negativity? Snap out of wishful thinking, because to make it through this life you're going to have to fight to overcome the "Inner-me" which is often our greatest enemy. You can't numb the pain with money, sex, drugs, clubs, people, or material possessions. You have to allow God to heal you from the nagging pain, or the crippling effects will destroy your life.

GROWING PAINS

Change takes growth and in order to grow, you will have to endure some growing pains. Yes, there will be setbacks, but you can bounce back. My life is proof, that every setback is a setup for your greatest comeback. It's positioning you for overcoming power.

I'm reminded of a quote which declares, "You never know how strong you are, until being strong is the only option." There is strength within you that you haven't used yet, because the situation has not presented itself, to unveil your level of strength. The power and strength that you have on the inside, can propel you beyond what you're facing on the outside.

Everybody in this life, will face challenges and endure struggle. On the contrary, it's not only about what you go through, it's how you handle what you go through. Life is experienced at a greater level when you can grow through, what you have to go through.

GROW THROUGH IT

It takes volition and an undying will, to endure the storm, dark clouds, rainy days, and trying times of life. You won't get to your goal by going under, around, or over the obstacle…you have to go through it, to get to it! Keep going and growing through life.

Never forget that the greater the obstacle, the greater the opportunity. This is not the time to breakdown, this is your time to breakthrough! The bigger your battle, the bigger your blessing! No matter, how great the odds are against you or how people have written you off, don't give up! Don't let a setback, set you back...bounce back! Eliminate negative self-talk, because what you say to yourself has a greater impact on you, than what people say to you.

FROM SETBACK TO COMEBACK

Many times, I share about being diagnosed with cancer at the age of fifteen. See when you share my story, that's journalism. When I personally share my story, it's a testimony of what God has done for me.

It was prayer, faith, and an unwavering will to live, which propelled me to press my way, towards total healing and victory. I'm blessed to be alive and convey these words to empower you. When you're facing a battle, you don't need worriers around you, but you need warriors to fight for you. My mother, Dr. Janice K. Connor was the prayer warrior in my life, who encouraged me to fight when I felt like giving up.

Don't fail to recognize that your setback, is only a setup for a comeback. Your struggle may not be cancer or a health related illness, it may be bitterness or depression. Your obstacle might be the loss of a relationship, divorce, financial woes, or someone who betrayed you. Whatever it is, overcome it, and bounce back from it!

PLEASURE VS. PAIN

Life brings changes, that we have to grind and grapple through, in order to birth our greatness. Since there is nothing to numb the pain of change, you're going to feel every stretching point and place of discomfort. Life comes with growing pains, simply because change hurts. There will be pain either way. It's either the pain of discipline or the pain of consequence.

The pain of discipline comes from doing what you don't want to do, yet staying true to the task at hand to see it through. The pain of consequence, comes from the refusal to do what you know to do and suffering the consequences as a result. When you know better, you have to do better. If you're waiting until you feel like doing it, you never will do it.

Don't seek pleasure, at the expense of ignoring a little pain. The right pain can break you through, the wrong pain can break you down. You may be crying, but don't stop moving forward. Yes, you may have been knocked down, but rise up and press your way through it.

We must become uncomfortable, with being comfortable and become comfortable, with being uncomfortable. Everyday we're in a fight between who we are, who we were, and who we have the potential to become. Don't let your past or present, become a prison that shackles your future. The past is a prison, but breaking out and walking in your future is freedom!

CHANGED, CHARGED, CONNECTED

It takes a changed and charged mindset, to break free from negativity. Just like your computer and phone needs to be charged, so too your mind must be charged and connected to a power source. If you're plugged into and connected to negativity, you won't have the energy and wisdom to sustain your life.

As the days, weeks, months, and years prolong, your strength and vitality will be depleted, if you're not connected to the right source. You will eventually become a product of who and what you're connected to, because of what you have become and attached yourself to.

Start disconnecting yourself from bad relationships, fear, gossip, depression, drama, and negative thinking.

Plug into the SOURCE of power, strength, peace, joy, hope, and love. As a result, you will have all of the RESOURCES, that you need to succeed in life.

OUT WITH THE OLD, IN WITH THE NEW

Indeed OLD habits die hard, but NEW habits can spring life into your spirit. Positive habits, invigorate you with hope and determination. The steps to change, is what it takes to see changes! You can't become all that you can be, by remaining all that you have been. Change will never happen TO you, if it first doesn't happen IN you.

This is your time to step into the best and blessed days of your life! Let healing and love, be your compass that guides you on the path of purpose, opening the door to your destiny! Realize that the greatest change comes, when you begin to think practically and willingly work to *Heal Your Heart*.

10 RELATIONSHIP TIPS

As a bonus, here are *10 tips to Live, Love, and Heal From Broken Relationships:*

1. Develop A Strong Relationship With God.

The greatest connection that you can have, is a relationship with God. He is the utmost eternal partner. When you have a spiritual foundation, you learn how to love yourself and others in a greater way.

The relationship or marriage will never work, if your relationship with God and your relationship with yourself, isn't developed first and foremost. God wants to do a new thing in you, but you have to trust Him and follow His direction. He gives you insight, through his Word but you have to communicate with Him. If you partner with Him, the blessings and benefits, are far beyond anything that you can imagine.

2. Grow And Get Better Everyday.

In order to grow and get better, you have to continually work to do it. Don't get lazy when it comes to putting in the work, to live your best life. There is no growth, without self-reflection and personal analysis. Self-development is the key that unlocks the door, to growth and opportunities.

In this world of distractions, it's important to take time to read, meditate, analyze your goals, and think. Growth brings with it growing pains, because change is uncomfortable. Sometimes it hurts to break away from bad habits and things you like to do, but know they aren't any good for you. As I mentioned before, it's either the pain of discipline or the pain of consequence. Ultimately, it's your decision.

3. Better Crew, Better You!

If the people that you're connected to aren't ADDING to your life, it's time to SUBTRACT them from your life. On your life journey, you don't need liabilities, you need assets! Distance yourself from people, who drain you of your time, energy, and patience.

There are some people in your life, that you must bless and release. Sometimes you have to love people from a distance. A better you, begins by surrounding yourself with a better crew of people. Why surround yourself with people, who only intend to kill your dream? They are only keeping you, in a place of negativity. Who you're connected to, determines what you're directed to. Disconnect yourself from negative people and get connected to those, who challenge you to be a better you.

4. Invest In Yourself.

Giving and investing, always creates room for more. It takes character to remain selfless, in a society of selfishness and self-aggrandizement. What you can give is more powerful, than what you can get and how you can get it. How many clothes and shoes, can you wear at one time? How many cars can you drive, all at once? We have become so inundated by what we can CONSUME, that we don't take the time to INVEST.

Make an investment in yourself and in the lives of others. What you can give may not be monetary, but it can be giving your time...which is far greater than money. Look within your relationships, around your community, and you will see that every problem has a solution that you can provide. There's always a blessing that comes, by blessing other people. You can give without loving, but you can't love without giving!

5. Step Into The Winner's Circle.

Whether you're in the winner's circle or not, depends on the people in your circle. You are who you hang around. You will either be a chicken or an eagle, a chump or a champion, a worrier or a warrior...which will you choose? You can't be a whiner and a winner at the same time!

Get out of the back seat of your life. Take responsibility, by getting in the drivers seat. Make a decision to press your way, towards the path of purpose and destiny. You can't win with a losers mentality. You will find yourself in the winners circle, when you step into a mindset of success.

6. Live Your Life, Like It's Golden.

A few years ago, Jill Scott released a song, *Golden*, which spoke to the value within, that shapes the world around you. You can't live your life like it's golden, if your mind is rusted. When you recognize the God-given treasure within, you will see the enormous value that permeates your life. Love yourself, respect, and value yourself through every negative circumstance and painful experience…there's a treasure in you!

You are blessed with gifts and talents, but the tragedy is when you never use, what you've been given. You are a red box and gold bow...you're a gift to the world. You must take personal inventory of your life and work your gifts.

How long will you procrastinate on your purpose? It's time to write the book, open the business, and develop your skill set. No one is going to hand you anything, you have to work to attain what you desire. Work your gifts! The best way to be found is by working, looking your best, and being the best that God made you to be.

7. Value You.

Invest in your value and become wealthy, from the inside out. You can never go bankrupt, when you invest in your value. Become wealthy from the inside out!

Having a beautiful exterior with nothing in your mind, is like having a *Louis Vuitton* bag with no money inside. Your value and worth doesn't begin from the outside-in, it starts from the inside-out. Your value isn't tied to what people think about you, it's in how you think about yourself. Get around people who enhance your value, avoid ones who diminish it. The more you value yourself, the more people will value you!

8. Let Go Of The Past.

You won't live your best life, until you let go of anger, bitterness, and strife. You can't change the past, so why are your presently living in it? You have to let it go, in order to grow.

Don't beat yourself up, over something you can't change. Let go of people, who continually hurt you. Stop reliving the memories of the past, that keep you living in the past. Release the past, so you can receive your future. It's over, get up and move your life forward!

9. Forgive To Live.

What are you holding onto, that's stifling your growth? There are certain pains that we have experienced, but we must forge ahead in spite of the hurt. Holding onto the past is a hindrance and hazard, to your hope and happiness.

There are some people in your life, who are stifling your progress and you have to let them go.

Some people that we connected to, were not good to or for us and we knew that. However, we decided to connect with those individuals anyway and got hurt in the process. The wrong people represent roadblocks to your purpose. The right people are a route to greatness. Choose your company wisely.

Life is about learning from our mistakes and moving forward, not repeating the same mistakes and living in the past. Don't take your past into your present and future. You can't be free for your future, if you're still a slave to your past. Your past will confine you, but only your future will release you.

Yes, we have been victims but we have also been perpetrators, of our own behavior. If God forgave you, then forgive yourself and forgive others. Let go of bitterness and brokenness. Seek to forgive and seek to be forgiven. Your bountiful living, is connected to the power of forgiving.

10. Love Yourself.

Too many times, we focus on our weaknesses and become so self-critical, that we ignore the strengths that we possess within. You can't expect anybody to love and appreciate who you are, if you don't love and appreciate yourself first.

You will eventually attract who and what you are, by the way you view and treat yourself. Know who you are and whose you are. When you don't know who you are, you leave it to the world to define you. Love yourself, embrace your uniqueness, and know your worth!

To all of the **QUEENS**…

A **QUEEN** speaks to the King in you. She nurtures, encourages, upgrades, and inspires you.

Her beauty resides not only on the OUTSIDE, it shines from the INSIDE. She knows her worth, being priceless from birth.

A **QUEEN** is more than her ASSETS, she is an ASSET. Look into the mirror of your soul, there's strength to press towards your goal.

Heal Your Heart and make a brand new start. There's no need to COMPETE, for a **QUEEN** is COMPLETE. So she COMPLEMENTS her COMPANION, forming a more perfect union.

In a world of QUANTITY,
you're a **QUEEN** of QUALITY!

Quintessentially
Unique
Empowering
Everyone
Naturally

ACKNOWLEDGMENTS

There is no way that I could write this book, without experiencing God's love in my life, to heal my bruises and bandage brokenness within. I truly thank God, for giving me the strength to write this literary exposé on love. The lessons learned and the information gained, have enriched my life as a result.

There are not enough pages to express my gratitude to mentors, teachers, colleagues, business partners, family, and friends. All of you have encouraged me and provided opportunities along the way. From the depths of my heart, I thank you.

I was blessed to witness one of the greatest relationships, that I have ever seen, through the 63-year marriage of my grandparents. Although my grandfather has passed on, I will never forget watching him treat my grandmother like a queen. He always referred to her as "Angel." I learned so much about love, just by observing how they treated one another.

My grandfather, Harry Smith, Jr. was a true inspiration to me and so many others. Sometimes all you have are the memories. A true father figure and hero to me, who served God, his family, and country with excellence. He left an indelible mark, that will never be erased. He led with love and so I cherish his life, leadership, and legacy.

As I wrote this book, my grandfather, was my guardian angel. I could feel his spirit, pushing and inspiring me to share a message of life, love, and healing for hurting hearts.

ABOUT THE AUTHOR

DR. EDDIE M. CONNOR, JR. is an author of the bestselling books, *Purposefully Prepared to Persevere, Collections of Reflections, Volumes 1-3: Symphonies of Strength, E.CON the ICON: from Pop Culture to President Barack Obama,* and *Unwrap The Gift In YOU!*

As a College Professor and International Speaker, Dr. Connor empowers people to overcome obstacles and walk in their unique purpose, by sharing his story of overcoming stage 4 cancer. He earned a Doctorate in Education and serves as Graduate Education Professor, at the prestigious Marygrove College.

Dr. Eddie M. Connor, Jr. is a recipient of the Dr. Martin Luther King, Jr. Humanitarian Award and has been featured on numerous media outlets including CBS, NBC, PBS, and The Word Network. He was nationally featured on the BET documentary, "It Takes A Village to Raise Detroit."

Dr. Connor speaks extensively on the subjects of education, healthy relationships, leadership, and maximizing your purpose. Much of his work extends throughout Jamaica and South Africa. He is also the founder of Boys 2 Books, which provides mentorship to young males via literacy, leadership, and life skills enrichment.